Spiritual Formation

INVITED TO FOLLOW

Student Workbook

Wheaton Press
Train. Equip. Reflect.

Spiritual Formation
Student Workbook

© 2010, 2013
Published by Wheaton Press
Wheaton, Illinois

www.WheatonPress.com

ISBN-13: 978-0615821498
ISBN-10: 0615821499

1. Christian Education – Discipleship 2. Spiritual Formation – Discipleship. 3. Christ-centered – Education.
4. Nonfiction-Religion and Spirituality-Christian Life. 5. Nonfiction-Spiritual Growth-Christ-centered.

Copyright and Trademark Standard

Accordingly, international and domestic laws and penalties guaranteeing patent, copyright, trademark, and trade secret protection safeguard the ideas, concepts, and recommendations related within this document.

Contact the publisher for discounted copies for partner schools and receive free resources and training for teachers.
Learn more at WheatonPress.com or email WheatonPress@gmail.com

FOR OUR STUDENTS.

FOLLOW ME

And I will make you…

Mark 1:17

Spiritual Formation

INVITED TO FOLLOW

Equipping Students to Reflect Christ

	YEAR ONE	YEAR TWO	YEAR THREE	YEAR FOUR
Growth Emphasis	An Emphasis on Believing	An Emphasis on Following	An Emphasis on Loving	An Emphasis on Going
Essential Questions	1. What does a healthy, mature follower of Christ believe? 2. How does a healthy, mature follower of Christ live?	3. How do I grow as a healthy, mature follower of Christ? 4. How do I equip others to grow as healthy, mature followers of Christ?	5. Who do others say Jesus is? 6. Who do I say Jesus is?	7. What do I believe? 8. Why do I believe? 9. How will I communicate to others?
Essential Outcomes	Understand and articulate Christ-centered beliefs	Develop authentic Christ-centered values	Develop and articulate a Christ-centered vision	Develop a clear Christ-centered personal mission
Courses	Foundations of Faith	Spiritual Formations Leadership, Evangelism, & Discipleship	Life of Christ Philosophy & Theology	Doctrine & Apologetics Christ & Culture

Class Overview

Essential Questions

1. How do I grow to reflect Christ in every area of my life?

2. How do I equip others to grow to reflect Christ?

Unit Essential Questions

1. What is the desired outcome of spiritual formation?

2. What is the path for spiritual growth?

3. How do I understand and apply Christ's invitation to repent?

4. How do I understand and apply Christ's invitation to believe?

5. How do I understand and apply Christ's invitation to follow?

6. How do I understand and apply Christ's invitation to love and deny?

7. How do I understand and apply Christ's invitation to go and teach?

Course Description

Students will understand that Christ's example in discipleship is the model for both the process of spiritual growth and the product of spiritual maturity. The stages of spiritual growth identified and utilized by Christ will be used as the outline for the course. Students will learn to apply the principles of spiritual growth taught by Christ and identify His model both personally and in the context of community.

Unit Learning Outcomes

A. Students will understand Christ's invitation to "follow me" and apply Him as the standard for spiritual maturity.

B. Students will evaluate the phrase "I will make you" and be able to articulate Christ's model for spiritual growth.

C. Students will evaluate and apply the implications of the Gospel to everyday life (Repent and Believe).

D. Students will learn to spend time with Jesus through the practice of personal spiritual disciplines (Follow Me).

E. Students will identify what it means to trust Jesus through personal trials and temptation (Deny Yourself).

F. Students will identify the implications and personal application for what it means to follow Christ in today's culture (Love and Obey).

G. Students will be challenged to activate their faith within their circles of influence (Fishers of Men).

H. Students will express and evaluate who they are and how God has uniquely developed them to impact and influence their circles of influence by adding their Faith Journey and Mentor Projects to their spiritual portfolio.

Class Overview

Essential Learning Skills

I. Students will gain tools such as writing, studying, thinking, discussing, presenting, and communicating through a Christ-centered worldview.

By the completion of this course students will be able to use scripture to:

A. Identify and describe the implications between a focus on the causes and a focus on the outcomes of spiritual growth in the lives of both individuals and communities.

B. Explain a clear definition of a healthy and spiritually mature reflection of Christ.

C. Explain a clear Christ-centered growth path with specific next steps for spiritual growth.

D. Prepare a personalized plan for spiritual growth and be able to reproduce the process through a disciple-making relationship.

E. Explain the principles of spiritual growth to an individual or small group and lead them through the process of creating and implementing a personalized plan for spiritual growth.

Unit 5   Believe.

    1.   Why did Jesus invite people to believe?

    2.   What is the Gospel?

    3.   What is the tension between discipleship and religion in Galatians 1-3?

    4.   What are the consequences of belief in Galatians 4-6?

    5.   How does what I believe impact how I live?

    6.   What does a mature follower of Christ believe?

Unit 6   Follow.

    1.   What is the Mentor Project?

    2.   What is the difference between believers and followers of Jesus?

    3.   How did Jesus disciple those who followed Him?

    4.   How do we recognize false teachers?

    5.   What is the role of spiritual disciplines in discipleship?

    6.   How do I embrace grace and connect to the power of the Holy Spirit?

Unit 7   Love and Deny.

    1.   What is the difference between being a follower and being a friend of Jesus?

    2.   What is the difference between a transformative cause and outcome?

    3.   How does Jesus use testing and trials as a part of the transformation process?

    4.   How does God use trials, temptations, and time to teach trust?

    5.   What is the role of community and accountability in transformation?

    6.   How do I live with joy in the midst of trials?

Unit 8   Go. Teach.

    1.   How do I share with others what God is doing in my life?

    2.   What is God doing in and through the lives of my classmates?

    3.   What are my next steps for growth?

Bible Memory Project

Due Dates

Ephesians 5:1	Due _____
Hebrews 4:12	Due _____
2 Timothy 3:16	Due _____
2 Timothy 2:15	Due _____
1 Corinthians 9:24-26	Due _____
John 1:14	Due _____
John 3:16-17	Due _____
1 Corinthians 15:1-6	Due _____
Romans 12:1-2	Due _____
Colossians 2:6-10	Due _____
James 1:2-4	Due _____
James 1:2-4	Due _____
Hebrews 12:1-13	Due _____

Spiritual Formation

Read through the following article and highlight or underline any parts that resonate with you. Then answer the reflection questions on the next page.

Not that I have already obtained all this, or have already arrived at my goal, but I press on to take hold of that for which Christ Jesus took hold of me.

Philippians 3:12 (NIV)

Invitations to Respond

To say it is intimidating to write a book about the path to spiritual maturity would be an understatement. It is only natural to wonder whether or not the principles presented on paper are actually present in the life of the author.

To that end, this book is as much a reflection of my own journey toward understanding how to apply Christ's invitations to my own life as it is an attempt to clearly convey them to others.

As my understanding of the invitations of Christ has grown, I have felt challenged to share them with others. Yet even as my desire to share them increased, I seemed unable to communicate them with simplicity. It was not uncommon to find myself sitting down to write, only to learn that the Lord needed to first refine things in my own life.

While frustrating at times, it is a foundational principle of how Christ views spiritual formation. He must be allowed to lead us into His reflection. We learn to respond to Him by offering all of ourselves to Him first.

The truth is that Jesus desires to work in us in order to work through us.

Jesus is still in the business of redemption and transformation.

Consider some of Christ's redemptive invitations throughout the Gospels.

When a man who was belittled throughout his life due to his short stature and his dishonorable profession heard that Christ was coming to town, he climbed up a tree to get a better view above the crowds. He hoped to catch a glimpse of the Messiah. Upon seeing the Lord, Zacchaeus received the invitation to come down, invite his friends, and have the honor of hosting Christ in his home for dinner (Luke 19:1-10).

When a woman caught in adultery and publically embarrassed by the religious leaders of her day found herself at the feet of the Messiah, instead of hearing Him condemn her for her sin, she received an invitation to experience a new life (John 8:1-11).

When young Jewish men were not qualified to study the Torah and follow a Rabbi, they learned their father's trade. Generally, they were not thought to be well-educated or qualified, yet Jesus' disciples were such men.

The same Jesus who invites a tax collector to respond to His invitation to dinner, who invites an adulteress to experience forgiveness and a new life, and who equips uneducated young men, is the same Jesus who invites you to respond to the invitation He has for you.

No matter what your past experience or current beliefs, the truth is that Jesus is still in the business of making disciples and transforming lives.

Jesus is still walking along the shores of our lives, and He is inviting us to stop what we are doing and to accept His invitation to follow where He leads.

Jesus desires for us to place our faith and trust in Him and in His plan for our life. He desires that we trust Him and His timing. He invites us to follow His path.

I don't know your spiritual story or what struggles you have faced in life, but He does.

I don't know the setbacks you have faced or the expectations that have not been met, but He does.

I don't know the people who have hurt or rejected you. I don't know the pain others may have caused that led you to doubt the goodness of God toward your life, but He does.

He is not unaware of your hurts, your fears, or your dreams, but He invites you to learn to hear His voice, accept His invitation, and follow His path to a life of transformation and healing.

Reflection

1.   Can you relate to any of the scenarios that the author is describing? If so, which ones and why?

2.   Explain the following statement in your own words;

> "The truth is that Jesus desires to work in us in order to work through us."

3.   Explain the following statement in your own words;

> "Jesus is still in the business of redemption as well as transformation."

Reflection

4. How would you currently describe your spiritual journey?

5. What are some of the concerns that you have as you consider taking this course?

6. What are some of the things that excite you as you consider taking this course?

7. What is one question or concern that you would like to address or answer through this course?

Spiritual Formation

Spiritual Formation

INVITED TO FOLLOW

Unit Essential Questions

1. What is the desired outcome of this class?

2. What do need to learn and what is my plan for learning?

Unit Learning Objectives

A. To understand the essential questions, learning objectives, and expectations of this class

B. To identify my personal learning needs

C. To develop a personalized learning plan for this class

D. To understand the difference between discipleship programs and Christ-centered discipleship

Unit Learning Assessments

1. Expectations for growth personal reflection handout

2. The Global Student Assessment

3. Final Exam Pre-Assessment

4. Personal Spiritual Formation Assessment

Daily Essential Questions

1. What is the learning goal for Spiritual Formation?

2. Why does spiritual formation matter?

3. What is expected of me in this class?

4. What are my personal goals for learning?

5. Where will we start as we examine how our faith is built?

Read through the following chapter and highlight or underline any parts that resonate with you or that that you have questions about and would like to discuss in class.

Expectations

Good Gifts

If there was an award for the worst Christmas present giver, I would win. Over the years, my family has learned that it is impossible for me to buy anyone a Christmas present until the very last minute. Perhaps some of the other men and women who are out shopping during the waning hours of Christmas Eve are there because they are too busy to shop earlier in the season, but my struggle is of a different kind.

It's not that I have a problem remembering dates or that I'm negligent in some way. My struggle is that whenever I find the perfect Christmas present for someone I love, I get so excited that I want to give it to them immediately. When I picture the smiles on their faces as they open their gifts, I find it impossible to wait until Christmas morning.

So I give them their gift as soon as I get home.

As you may imagine, this tends to cause problems. When all of the gifts have been opened several weeks before Christmas, the tree has the potential to seem empty on Christmas morning.

Imagine what it might be like to wake up on Christmas morning and realize that the presents under the tree are actually the same gifts that your dad gave you a few weeks earlier, rewrapped for effect.

One year, in an attempt to demonstrate to my family that I could exercise some level of self-discipline, I went shopping the weekend before Christmas determined to keep the gifts a surprise for the three days that remained before Christmas morning.

My plan didn't work.

I could not wait even one day.

I was so excited that in spite of a joint effort on their behalf to resist me, I eventually wore the rest of the family down and by the end of the night had convinced each of my daughters to open their presents.

My problem with gift giving is so bad that when I do come home with the gifts in the car, typically on the day before Christmas, my children will actually run away from me to ensure that I do not try to give them their gifts before morning.

I cannot help myself.

I love giving gifts to my kids!

Sometimes I wonder if this is how God feels about us.

The Bible says that He loves giving good gifts to his children.

> *"If you then, though you are evil, know how to give good gifts to your children, how much more will your Father in heaven give good gifts to those who ask him!"*
> *Matthew 7:11 (NIV)*

Take a moment and remember the last time Christmas morning was exciting for you. When you were a kid, did you ever feel like the most difficult task in life was falling asleep on Christmas Eve? Did you ever feel so much anticipation and excitement that it seemed impossible to hold still long enough to actually close your eyes?

Yet, as difficult as it was to fall asleep, it was always so easy to wake up in anticipation of Christmas morning.

God's gifts are perfect

As a parent, I love watching my children run down the stairs on Christmas morning as I invite them to receive the gifts that were purchased with them in mind.

But if that feeling is the reflection of my imperfect heart, then I confess I can't even begin to fathom or explain how our perfect, heavenly Father feels towards us as He personally invites each of us to respond to His invitation to follow Him and to receive His best desires for our lives.

John 10:10 records that Jesus said, " I have come that you may have life, and have it to the full."

The New Living Translation translates His words as "My purpose is to give them a rich and satisfying life."

God's gift of a transformed life of rich, satisfying fullness is given out of love. It is something that He desires for us to experience.

It is not temporary. It does not lose value or gather dust and rust in a garage. It is an invitation to an eternal transformation.

It is a gift that is not cheap either. It was not purchased at the last minute or at a discount. It is a gift that cost Him everything through the death of Christ on the cross.

It is this same God who invites us to trust that His desire for us to experience an abundant life of transformation is not available to everyone who calls Him Father and not only to a select few.

Reflection.

Describe what you think of when you think of the concept of spiritual growth or transformation? Do you view it as a gift from a loving father or from a different perspective?

Describe what you think has influenced your opinion or perspective of God's view toward you?

How would your life be different if you believed that God's invitations for a transformed life was the invitation of a loving Father who desired to give you a priceless gift?

What do you think it would take for you to believe that?

Some Assembly Required

Amidst all the excitement and nostalgia of Christmas, I have learned there are four things that have the potential to ruin an otherwise perfect Christmas morning.

The first are the words, "Batteries not included," coupled with a realization that I do not have enough batteries.

While a few missing batteries can make me feel foolish, it is a dilemma that can be solved with a quick trip to a gas station.

The second thing that can put a crimp on the morning is the number of twisty ties, layers of packing tape, and other security gizmos that need to be untwisted, sawed and hacked through in order to free a doll and her accessories from the prison of her packaging.

I honestly think it may be easier to break a prisoner out of a maximum-security prison than it is to spring a doll free from her package. But, with a Swiss Army knife, a hacksaw, and a bit of determination, it is still possible.

It is the third issue, however, that causes me to feel completely inadequate as both a parent and a human.

It is the phrase "some assembly required," coupled with an obscure set of directions that seem to be written for a PhD candidate that can ruin what, up until that moment, was a wonderful Christmas morning.

In addition to my struggle waiting to give gifts until Christmas morning, I also struggle doing anything that involves directions, tools and my hands.

My struggle in this area is also not a secret to those who know me well. At my bachelor party, I received an incredibly elaborate set of tools and a really nice box to put them in with a card that read, "For your wife."

And over the past twenty years, my wife has gotten a lot of use out of them.

There are few things that make me feel worse about my lack of ability in this area than sitting on the floor with a set of directions, an assortment of random parts, and a bunch of tools that I have absolutely no idea how to use to assemble a gift for someone that I love.

I typically experience seven recognizable stages of emotion in these types of situations. The first stage consists of twinges of inadequacy and embarrassment coupled with fleeting thoughts of "Oh no, not again!"

The second stage is marked by a renewed determination as my internal monologue rationalizes my previous failures as a lack of effort.

Throughout this stage, I attempt to convince myself that this time will be different if I simply try harder. This stage usually involves opening up all of the small packages and laying the pieces out neatly on the floor around me.

The third stage is the moment when I am forced to acknowledge reality. It involves reading the directions multiple times and trying to make sense out of the cryptic words and pictures in front of me in hopes that they will begin to make sense, but slowly realizing that no matter how loud, soft, fast, or slow, I am no where closer to understanding or progressing in any meaningful way.

Then, as I continue to sit and stare at the directions, I slowly find myself morphing into the fourth stage, as my mind begins to fill with all of the possible synonyms for the word, "incomprehensible." Words like 'obscure,' 'mysterious,' 'impenetrable,' 'cryptic,' 'arcane,' 'secret,' 'deep,' 'hidden,' 'esoteric,' and 'unknowable' all flood my mind as my anxiety increases and my frustration becomes more difficult to hide.

Next is the fifth stage, which involves a certain level of finger pointing. Sometimes the finger is pointed at the nameless person who wrote the directions while other times I find it pointed back at myself and my growing sense of frustration and inadequacy.

At the sixth stage, I embrace the reality of my failure. It is here that I remember Einstein's insight that doing the same thing over and over while expecting different results is the definition of insanity. I realize my own momentary madness of believing that trying harder would have brought about a different result. I give in to feelings of hopelessness and anger.

It is at that moment, in spite of my best intentions and effort, as my physical and mental exhaustion overtakes me, I slump into the seventh stage and resign myself to accepting my failure.

For some of us, these stages and emotions may feel like descriptions of our attempts to decipher the directions within our personal spiritual journey.

At some point in our life, we were presented with the amazing gift of salvation and the new life that is available through Jesus Christ. We embraced the truth that it is not by any works we could do, but by God's grace and through faith in the shed blood of Jesus that we are forgiven of our sin and justified before God.

Some of us felt nothing while others may have experienced a moment of peace, delight or even joy when we received God's gift of salvation and forgiveness.

Then, armed with Christ's promise that we could experience life to the full we set out to learn how to live a life that pleased God as if it was a present waiting for us to unwrap.
With all of the energy and tenacity of a new believer, we tackled the project of growing in our relationship with Christ with anticipation and expectation. We opened the Bible, attended church, bought the latest Christian book, and tuned our radios to the Christian station.

 But the truth is that for many of us, this project of spiritual growth and transformation ended up being more difficult than anticipated.

And at some point, we realized that the process of growing in our relationship with God carried with it the label, "some assembly required."

For example, after purchasing our first Bible, we opened it up and then wondered how to read it. Where were we supposed to start?

The sermons we heard at church did not always seem to engage or challenge us. The book that a friend promised would change our lives and "speak to our hearts" might have failed to deliver. And the week that we decided to listen to our local Christian radio station happened to be the week they were raising money to meet their budget.

In spite of all of our willingness and desire, somehow the directions on how that process was actually supposed to take place seemed obscure, mysterious, and unknowable.

But, lest we gain the false belief that it is simply new believers, or just a few rare outliers, who have struggled with understanding the directions for spiritual growth, a number of recent studies have confirmed large numbers of people who have learned that busyness does not equate to holiness.

People like you and me who longed for change but often fell into a pattern of Christian activity without experiencing Christ-centered victory.

Perhaps you can relate to the frustration of thinking that regular church attendance, small group involvement, a service project, an evening of worship, or even giving more money would open the door and usher you into lasting spiritual change only to discover that even those activities failed to produce enduring fruit in your life.

If you can relate to even one of these scenarios, then I have two messages for you. First, you are not alone. Second, do not lose hope.

Pause and Reflect – What has been my experience?

1. Can I relate to any of those scenarios? Have there been times when I have felt frustrated or confused about what direction to take in your own spiritual journey? Explain your answer.

2. Do I know anyone else who has experienced something similar?
   If so, what would I tell them?

Shared Experience

Over 20 years ago, I thought it was just me that struggled with the concept of spiritual growth.

Somehow I had managed to grow up in the church, attend a Bible college, become a pastor of adult discipleship at a large church, and yet, when I was alone in my office, I was not sure if I knew what it meant to be discipled by someone else, let alone what it meant to equip a church of people to become disciple makers.

Changing the Rules

For nearly a decade, I read books, interviewed others, and even conducted leadership training on the topic of discipleship all the while deep down inside, feeling like I was playing a game of *"Calvin Ball"* with God when it came to the topic of personal discipleship and personal disciple making.

In case you are not familiar with the term, "Calvin Ball," let me start by pointing out that it is not intended to be a reference to a theological system of belief, and it is in no way attached to the theologian John Calvin.

Rather, Calvin Ball is a game that was popularized by the comic strip Calvin and Hobbes™. The comic is about the adventures of a young boy named Calvin and his imaginary friend, a stuffed tiger named Hobbes.

When adults are not around, Hobbes comes to life, and he and Calvin enjoy many fantastic adventures together. One of their favorite games is a made-up game they call "Calvin Ball."

Calvin Ball is an interesting game to attempt to describe, understand, and play. The key to the game is understanding and playing by the two rules of Calvin Ball.

Rule 1

You can never play the game the same way twice.

Rule 2

Anyone can add or change rules at any time.

One of my favorite comic strips is when Calvin scores what he believes is the winning point. As he celebrates his perceived victory, he notices that instead of admitting defeat, Hobbes is celebrating as well. In fact, after calling a timeout, Hobbes actually claims to have won the game. Calvin protests by explaining that he had scored the winning goal.

But Hobbes quickly points out that Calvin had broken rule number one. He had scored a point by crossing the finish line in the same way that he had already done earlier in the game.

The result was that Calvin's efforts end up scoring the winning points for the other team. Calvin hangs his head in defeat and wonders why he bothers to play as Hobbes celebrates with a victory dance.

For many years discipleship felt a lot like Calvin Ball to me.

Sometimes it felt as though the rules were cryptic and ever changing. Sometimes it seemed, in the midst of being told that I needed to be a disciple of Christ, I was not told exactly how that process was supposed to take place.

Perhaps you can relate, or you know someone in your circle of influence who has told you their story of how, after all of their longing for change and several false starts, rule changes, or failed attempts, they threw up their hands in frustration and wondered why they even bothered to try at all.

After experiencing this process first hand and witnessing it in the lives of numerous others, I am convinced that this feeling of frustration is one of the factors that leads to the type of spiritual apathy noted by the author of Hebrews when he said:

"We have much to say about this, but it is hard to make it clear to you because you no longer try to understand. In fact, though by this time you ought to be teachers, you need someone to teach you the elementary truths of God's word all over again. You need milk, not solid food!"

Hebrews 5:11-12 (NIV)

How about you?

Can you relate to the audience of Hebrews? Have you reached a point where you have stopped trying to understand? Have you ever wrestled with the temptation to give up on experiencing growth or transformation in your life as a result of a personalized relationship with God?

As someone who has now been involved in discipleship and pastoral ministry for over two decades, I have met a lot of people who have stopped trying to understand. And while there are many reasons, over the years I began to see a couple of patterns emerging through the stories that I heard.

Some conventional models of spiritual growth emphasize the idea that when we gather on Sundays, go to small group meetings during the week, and give time, talent, and treasure, we are part of the process of discipleship.

This concept of being a disciple is can be presented as an invitation to become involved.

- We are invited to become involved as a member of a church.

- We are invited to become involved as a member of a small group.

- We are invited to become involved by serving in a ministry.

In a similar manner, the concept of becoming a disciple maker has been presented as inviting someone else to join you as you increase your involvement together.

Yet, in spite of our best efforts to get involved, or to invite others to increase their involvement, eventually we realize that our increased activity leaves us feeling more tired than transformed.

Then, after experiencing the exhaustion of trying to grow in our relationship with Christ and arriving at busyness rather than holiness, we get tired… and stop trying.

In the midst of all of the invitations to get more involved, there is another conventional pattern of thought that leads to spiritual exhaustion.

This conventional approach is built around the concept that spiritual maturity is when we try harder to smile more and swear less.

A recent poll discovered that 80 percent of Americans have come to believe that spiritual maturity is simply, "trying harder to do the right things."[1]

I can relate to that statistic.

When I was a kid, I thought the path to spiritual maturity meant I was supposed to pay attention in Sunday school, stay awake in church, and make sure not to get my church clothes wrinkled or dirty when I played outside on Sunday afternoons. It also meant I was supposed to try really hard to pay attention to the missionary who spoke during the Sunday service.

Later, as I got into high school, spiritual maturity seemed to be defined by ensuring that I did not smoke, drink, take drugs, or have premarital sex. If I could read my Bible at least five minutes a day, that would be a bonus!

Perhaps you read this and something inside of you resonates. In spite of all of your effort, there is something missing. You feel like there is supposed to be something more. Yet you are not exactly sure what you are supposed to be looking for or feeling.

Perhaps some of you have dared to turn to a trusted friend or a pastor and with great courage, you asked, "What am I missing?" only to be met with a less than satisfactory answer.

About ten years ago, I attended a leadership conference with tens of thousands of pastors and church staff in attendance. One speaker explained that at their church, the path to spiritual growth was to gather on Sunday for worship, get involved in a small group throughout the week, and to give of their time, talent, and treasure through service at the church.

All of these are great things by the way, but as I listened, I wondered if these activities were the path to spiritual growth or simply a path to deeper involvement?

As I listened to the speaker, he went on to share a conversation he had with a gentleman after one of his Sunday morning services.

He recounted the story of how this man had approached him and said he had taken all three steps, but still did not feel he was growing in his relationship with Christ. He wanted to know what he was missing.

I waited with baited breath for what I hoped would be the key, not only for the courageous man in the story, but also for myself and the rest of the leaders in attendance.

I was shocked when the speaker shared his response. He said, "That's all there is. If you need something else, then you better look to some other church, because that's what we do here."

I was stunned.

Both by the story itself and by the thunderous applause from the pastors around me. I cannot imagine what was going through the mind of the man who received that response.

Was he to believe that all of his involvement and efforts to busy himself about the work of spiritual growth were for nothing? Was he to believe that the secrets to spiritual growth were above his capacity or that God was withholding something from him in spite of his best efforts to be involved and to modify his behavior?

Was the man who desired to grow in his relationship with Christ left to simply to walk away from his pastor and think to himself, "Well, too bad for me?"

He had played by all the rules and did all the right things, yet he still felt something was missing.

Something felt incomplete. He was not sure what the final destination was supposed to be, and he was exhausted from his efforts to find out.

At this point in his process, the man was left with two options – either he needed to change churches or lower his expectations.

These two options leave us with to potential results that, like a virus, spreads throughout our body and infects every part of us. The results are pride or despair.

When we begin to believe that involvement and behavior modification lead to maturity, we make room for the virus of pride and despair.

Pride begins to take root and sometimes sounds like this; "Perhaps I simply need to lower my expectations. The truth is that God is actually pretty lucky to have me on His team. After all, I'm a pretty good person. I participate in a lot of different activities and I try hard to follow the rules."

Despair occurs when we check off the last thing on our list and we still feel empty, hollow, and exhausted inside. Despair sets in when we look at the list in front of us and realize we can never measure up. We can never be good enough. We cannot figure out why God will not bless our efforts to try harder or why He will not give an answer or even a little bit of direction.

While we look like we have it all together on the outside, deep down we feel we are in the middle of a game of *Calvin Ball,* and the game is not fun anymore.

Despair leads to anger. We grow angry with ourselves and with God. After all, why would He tell us to go and make disciples if He was going to make it so hard to understand the directions?

Does God not realize we want to grow and change, that we just need Him to point us in the right direction, and to help us understand what we are supposed to do?

And why would I want to have a relationship or invite anyone else to experience a relationship with a God who seemingly fails in such a significant way?

Does any of this sound familiar?

It did to me.

After years of activity, involvement, and attempts to to modify behavior, I had arrived at all of those conclusions and was finally confronted with the question, "Was God mean?"

Is God Mean?

I am convinced that one of the reasons so many people have stagnated, plateaued, or ultimately dropped out of many of our churches is that we have quietly become convinced that God is playing a mean trick on us.

Perhaps you are one of the people who have felt that you are missing something in you relationship with Christ and hoped that a change of location would fill their void.

Perhaps you share the experience where you have hoped that a new church, new pastor, new mission statement, new building, or new program would jump start your relationship with Christ and allow you to experience the change you longed for.

Determined to try harder, you prayed that the new idem would provide the catalyst for change, only to discover yourself returning to their same insane patterns of the past.

Some of us have repeated the cycle again and again until our disappointment grew into disillusionment, and after several attempts, some have eventually grown tired and quit trying altogether.

Perhaps this pattern is one of the factors that is contributing to the rise of the "nones" in our generation.

"Nones" are the roughly 23% of the population in the United States who statistically refer to themselves as having no religious affiliation. A number that increases to 38% of those who were born between 1981-1996.[2]

After interviewing pastors and church members from around the world, I am convinced that each Sunday there are men and women staying home from church, not because they have stopped loving Jesus, but because they are wrestling with the belief that either God is mean or that Jesus has stopped loving them.

To be honest, for a number of years, I struggled with the temptation of believing God is mean. I had heard that discipleship is one of the main responsibilities of being a Christian. I had heard sermons preached on how I am supposed to "go and make disciples."

Yet, after a lifetime within the walls of the church, I had no idea how to accomplish that task. It was as if it was Christmas morning and I was standing by the tree looking at the best gift ever without being able to understand the directions.

It was partially because of this personal crisis of faith that, after becoming a pastor, I dedicated myself to designing a discipleship plan that would provide understandable directions for myself and for those I was entrusted to shepherd. I spent years reading, researching, and attending every conference I could afford to attend.

But after trying multitudes of different programs, I felt like I was still living in the middle of a game of *Calvin Ball*. It seemed to me that every author had a different program to pitch or a different set of rules they were inviting others to play by, and yet I still could not define or figure out what the end goal was or how I was supposed to get there.

Examine for Yourselves

I remember attending church one Sunday in the midst of my search and listening to a pastor exhort his congregation to "get into the game" and make disciples. He went so far as to strongly insist we were "*living in sin*" if we were not "*in the game.*" But when the hype died down, he offered no instructions on how to actually play the game.

One day a few years later as I reflected on the experience, the word "abuse" came to mind. To demand that people accomplish something without helping them to understand the directions seems abusive.

I found myself questioning God.

Is God abusive? Is He asking something from us while at the same time hiding His directions?

The Bible is clear that our God is a loving God who enjoys giving good gifts to His children. The God of the Bible would find no pleasure or joy in arbitrarily withholding the directions from us.

It was shortly after this time that I stopped reading other people's books. "Enough of the insanity," I thought to myself. If Jesus wants us to go and make disciples, then He must have shown us how we are supposed to do it.

As I took out my Bible and found the familiar words in Matthew 4:19, I fixated on the first two words of Christ's invitation to His potential disciples: "Follow Me."

Perhaps this is not simply an invitation to the 12 disciples. Perhaps the summons to follow Jesus is a call to me too. Perhaps my job is not to design a discipleship program or plan; rather, my responsibility is first to follow Jesus.

Then I looked at the next five words,

"…and I will make you."

In the same way that Jesus is the one who made disciples in the Gospels, He is still the one making disciples today. Instead of designing a program for God, it is more important to look to Jesus and allow Him to work in and through us.

It was at that point that I experienced a new type of resignation. This time I was not seeking another promise or program created by a pastor, church leader, or even myself. Rather, I resigned from my need to help God, and I embraced the opportunity to seek the Word of God for His process and His set of directions.

I told God that I was through with the insanity of reading everyone else's books and manuals, and I was going to put Him to the test. No longer would I look outside the pages of Scripture for His process of making disciples. Instead, I was determined for God to reveal His process through the pages of Scripture.

This book is the result of that moment of resignation to God. I believe He does reveal His instructions for discipleship and disciple making in the Gospels. Even today, He is still the one who changes lives when we follow Him and respond to His invitations.

God loves to give gifts to His children. He invites us to engage His Word and His Spirit to discover His will and His directions.

This class is based on the discovery of a series of invitations given by Jesus that will equip you to discover His process for lasting spiritual transformation that leads to spiritual growth and maturity.

You are encouraged to examine the Biblical text for yourself to see if what is being presented actually matches what is revealed through the pages of Scripture. I remind my students regularly of the apostle Paul's words to the Bereans commending them for not simply believing Him, but for searching the Scriptures for themselves to determine God's answers.

> *"Now the Berean Jews were of more noble character than those in Thessalonica, for they received the message with great eagerness and examined the Scriptures every day to see if what Paul said was true."*
>
> *Acts 17:11 (NIV)*

I invite you to use this resource and the Scriptures contained within as a springboard for your own process of searching the Scripture and wrestling with the ideas that are presented. Ask God to give you wisdom and discernment as you read each Bible passage in the context in which God originally presented it.

I want to encourage you with two verses from the book of James. The first is found near the beginning of the first chapter:

> *"If any of you needs wisdom to know what you should do, you should ask God, and he will give it to you. God is generous to everyone and doesn't find fault with them."*
>
> *James 1:5 (GW)*

If you have been asking God for wisdom and you desire to grow in your relationship with Him, then there is a good chance you can relate to these words from James.

Perhaps you are looking for insight to help you through a difficult time.

Perhaps you are trying to make sense of a particular situation.

Maybe you have hit a plateau in your relationship with God and you want to move forward. Regardless of your motivation, you are asking God for a better understanding of where you are and where you are headed.

Jesus invites you to follow Him, and He promises He has the power to change you.

Second, let me encourage you with a verse found at the end of the letter from James where we are reminded:

> *"Elijah was a human being, even as we are."*
>
> *James 5:17 (NIV)*

It is through this simple verse that we are reminded that the very same God who answered Elijah's prayer that it would not rain also desires to answer your prayers for wisdom and direction in your journey to become an imitator of Him.

In light of that, take a moment and ask the God who loves to give good gifts and the God who answered the prayer of Elijah to give you wisdom and courage to hear and respond to His voice as you seek to follow Him.

Citations

1. "Many Churchgoers and Faith Leaders Struggle to Define Spiritual Maturity." Barna Group. May 11, 2009. https://www.barna.org/barna-update/article/12-faithspirituality/264-many-churchgoers-and-faith-leaders-struggle-to-define-spiritual-maturity#.VRI-SkYhw80.

2. 1http://www.pewresearch.org/fact-tank/2015/05/13/a-closer-look-at-americas-rapidly-growing-religious-nones/

Reflection and Application

My Story

Through this article the author shared his story, but what is yours?

What parts could you relate to? What parts of your story are similar? What parts are different?

In your own words, why does this class matters?

Why does a conventional approach to spiritual formation feel so overwhelming?

What do you hope to get out of this class?

My best class ever

Part I. Individual

1. What was the best class that I have ever been a part of?

2. What made it the best class that ever?

3. What did the teacher do to make it the best class ever?

4. What did I do to make it the best class ever?

5. What did the other students in the class do to make it the best class ever?

Part II. Pair and Share

1. Three ideas that I heard from someone else that I really liked include:

2. One thing that I think we should commit to as a class in order to make this the best class ever would be:

Examine ™

SPIRITUAL FORMATION TOOL

ChristCenteredDiscipleship.com

Everyone ought to examine themselves before
they eat of the bread and drink from the cup.
1 Corinthians 11:28

WP Wheaton Press
Train. Equip. Reflect.

Where are you?
Read. Respond. Reflect.

Directions: Read through the verses below and highlight or underline any words or phrases that seem to reflect or resonate with where you are at.

Skeptic. Presented with the person of Christ and the Gospel multiple times, I demonstrate disinterest or unbelief.

"Even after Jesus had performed so many signs in their presence, they still would not believe in him." John 12:37, NIV

Characteristics: Calloused heart, dull ears, closed eyes.

"[F]or this people's heart has grown callous, their ears are dull of hearing, they have closed their eyes." Matthew 13:15a,

Christ's Next-Step Invitation: Repent. Believe.

"Then he began to denounce the cities in which most of his mighty works had been done, because they didn't repent." Matthew 11:20 ,WEB

Growth Barrier: A lack of spiritual understanding.

"When anyone hears the message about the kingdom and does not understand it, the evil one comes and snatches away what was sown in their heart. This is the seed sown along the path." Matthew 13:19, NIV

Spiritual Need: A change of mind and heart initiated by the Holy Spirit, a loving and praying friend.

"He said to them, 'This kind can come out by nothing, except by prayer and fasting.'" Mark 9:29, WEB

"As for you, you were dead in your transgressions and sins, in which you used to live when you followed the ways of this world and of the ruler of the kingdom of the air, the spirit who is now at work in those who are disobedient." Ephesians 2:1-2, NIV

Seeker. Questioning, with a desire to learn more about Jesus.

"He answered, 'And who is he, sir? Tell me, so that I may believe in him.'" John 9:36, ISV

Characteristics: A ready heart, open ears, questions with an interest to learn more about Jesus.

"Again, the next day, John was standing with two of his disciples, and he looked at Jesus as he walked, and said, 'Behold, the Lamb of God!' The two disciples heard him speak, and they followed Jesus. Jesus turned, and saw them following, and said to them, 'What are you looking for?' They said to him, 'Rabbi' (which is to say, being interpreted, Teacher), 'where are you staying?' He said to them, 'Come, and see.' They came and saw where he was staying, and they stayed with him that day. It was about the tenth hour." John 1:35-39, WEB

Christ's Next-Step Invitation: Repent. Believe.

"Now after John was taken into custody, Jesus came into Galilee, preaching the Good News of God's Kingdom, and saying, 'The time is fulfilled, and God's Kingdom is at hand! Repent, and believe in the Good News.'" Mark 1:14-15, WEB

Growth Barrier: A lack of clear presentation and understanding of the Gospel, a lack of invitation.

"How, then, can people call on someone they have not believed? And how can they believe in someone they have not heard about? And how can they hear without someone preaching?" Romans 10:14, ISV

Spiritual Need: A clear Gospel presentation and an invitation to believe and receive salvation.

"But to all who did receive him, who believed in his name, he gave the right to become children of God." John 1:12, ESV

Believer. Presented with the Gospel I believe.

"He said, 'Lord, I believe!' and he worshiped him." John 9:38, WEB

Characteristics: Seed begins to germinate, shallow soil, little or no roots.

Other seeds fell on rocky ground, where they did not have much soil, and immediately they sprang up, since they had no depth of soil, but when the sun rose they were scorched. And since they had no root, they withered away. Matthew 13:5-6

Christ's Next-Step Invitation: Follow.

"And he said to them, 'Follow me, and I will make you fishers of men.'" Matthew 4:19, ESV

Growth Barrier: Lack of roots, lack of knowledge, testing, trouble, persecution.

"These in the same way are those who are sown on the rocky places, who, when they have heard the word, Immediately receive it with joy. They have no root in themselves, but are short-lived. When oppression or persecution arises because of the word, immediately they stumble. " Mark 4:16-17, WEB

Spiritual Need: Prayer, roots, knowledge, biblical teaching, time, worship and someone to walk with them.

"Like newborn infants, long for the pure spiritual milk, that by it you may grow up into salvation." I Peter 2:2, ESV

"So then, just as you received Christ Jesus as Lord, continue to live your lives in him, rooted and built up in him, strengthened in the faith as you were taught, and overflowing with thankfulness." Colossians 2:6-7, NIV

"We continually ask God to fill you with the knowledge of His will through all the wisdom and understanding that the Spirit gives, so that you may live a life worthy of the Lord and please Him in every way: bearing fruit in every good work, growing I n the knowledge of God, being strengthened with all power according to His glorious might so that you may have great endurance and patience, and giving joyful thanks to the Father, who has qualified you to share in the inheritance of His holy people in the kingdom of light." Colossians 1:9-12, NIV

Follower. Growing in faith and love; deepening roots and knowledge; struggling with thorns, trials, forgiveness, doubt, and perseverance.

"By this all people will know that you are my disciples, if you have love for one another." John 13:35, ESV

Characteristics: Beginning to push through the soil, struggling with thorns and weeds.

"Others fell among thorns. The thorns grew up and choked them." Matthew 13:7, WEB

"And calling the crowd to him with his disciples, he said to them, 'If anyone would come after me, let him deny himself and take up his cross and follow me.'" Mark 8:34, ESV

Christ's Next-Step Invitation: Deny self; pick up cross; trust, obey, and love Christ and others.

"Then Jesus said to his disciples, "If anyone desires to come after me, let him deny himself, and take up his cross, and follow me." Matthew 16:24, WEB

Growth Barrier: Thorns, worries of this life, doubt, deceitfulness of wealth, comfort, self and self-will.

"Others are those who are sown among the thorns. These are those who have heard the word, and the cares of this age, and the deceitfulness of riches, and the lusts of other things entering in choke the word, and it becomes unfruitful." Mark 4:18-19

Spiritual Need: Deny self; trials; endurance, perseverance, time, small group relationships, and accountability.

"Consider it pure joy, my brothers and sisters, whenever you face trials of many kinds, because you know that the testing of your faith produces perseverance. Let perseverance finish its work so that you may be mature and complete, not lacking anything." James 1:2-4, NIV

"Through him we have also obtained access by faith into this grace in which we stand, and we rejoice in hope of the glory of God. Not only that, but we rejoice in our sufferings, knowing that suffering produces endurance, and endurance produces character, and character produces hope." Romans 5:2-4, ESV

"These have come so that the proven genuineness of your faith—of greater worth than gold, which perishes even though refined by fire—may result in praise, glory and honor when Jesus Christ is revealed." 1 Peter 1:7, NIV

Friend. Marked by obedient love for Christ and others; may wrestle with isolation, complacency and accountability.

"You are my friends if you do what I command you." John 15:14, ESV

Characteristics: Good soil, obedience to Christ, fruit, growing faith, increasing love and perseverance in trials.

"We ought always to thank God for you, brothers and sisters, and rightly so, because your faith is growing more and more, and the love all of you have for one another is increasing. Therefore, among God's churches we boast about your perseverance and faith in all the persecutions and trials you are enduring." 2 Thessalonians 1:3-4, NIV

Christ's Next-Step Invitation: Love, obey, go, teach.

"If you love me, you will keep my commandments." John 14:15, ESV

"Jesus came to them and spoke to them, saying, 'All authority has been given to me in heaven and on earth. Go, and make disciples of all nations, baptizing them in the name of the Father and of the Son and of the Holy Spirit, teaching them to observe all things that I commanded you. Behold, I am with you always, even to the end of the age.' Amen." Matthew 28:18-20

Growth Barrier: Complacency, fear, pride, lack of vision and lack of equipping.

"Then he said to his disciples, 'The harvest indeed is plentiful, but the laborers are few.'" Matthew 9:37, WEB

"How, then, can people call on someone they have not believed? And how can they believe in someone they have not heard about? And how can they hear without someone preaching?" Romans 10:14, ISV

Spiritual Need: Vision, continued obedience, equipping, empowerment, continued spurring and accountability within community.

"...to equip his people for works of service, so that the body of Christ may be built up until we all reach unity in the faith and in the knowledge of the Son of God and become mature, attaining to the whole measure of the fullness of Christ." Eph 4:12-13

"As for you, brothers, do not grow weary in doing good." 2 Thessalonians 3:13, ESV

"Let us continue to hold firmly to the hope that we confess without wavering, for the one who made the promise is faithful. And let us continue to consider how to motivate one another to love and good deeds, not neglecting to meet together, as is the habit of some, but encouraging one another even more as you see the day of the Lord coming nearer." Hebrews 10:23-25, ISV

Fisherman. Reflecting Christ and reproducing fruit of righteousness and good works.

"Because we have heard of your faith in Christ Jesus and of the love you have for all God's people—the faith and love that spring from the hope stored up for you in heaven and about which you have already heard in the true message of the Gospel that has come to you. In the same way, the Gospel is bearing fruit and growing throughout the whole world—just as it has been doing among you since the day you heard it and truly understood God's grace." Colossians 1:4-6, NIV

Characteristics: Good soil, fruitfulness, harvest, influence, reflecting Christ.

"Others fell on good soil, and yielded fruit: some one hundred times as much, some sixty, and some thirty." Matthew 13:8

Christ's Next-Step Invitation: Teach others.

"Therefore, as you go, disciple people in all nations, baptizing them in the name of the Father, and the Son, and the Holy Spirit, teaching them to obey everything that I've commanded you." Matthew 28:19-20a, ISV

Growth Barrier: Complacency, fear, pride, lack of vision, lack of equipping, weariness.

"Let's not get tired of doing what is good, for at the right time we will reap a harvest—if we do not give up." Galatians 6:9, ISV

"Think about the one who endured such hostility from sinners, so that you may not become tired and give up." Hebrews 12:3,

Spiritual Need: Perseverance, humility, faithfulness, accountability, reliable people.

"It gave me great joy when some believers came and testified about your faithfulness to the truth, telling how you continue to walk in it." 3 John 3, NIV

"And what you have heard from me in the presence of many witnesses entrust to faithful men who will be able to teach others also." 2 Timothy 2:2, ESV

Examine™ Spiritual Formation Planning Tool

More resources available at WheatonPress.com

Directions: Answer the following seven questions using the words or phrases you highlighted or underlined.

1. Where am I?
   Skeptic. When presented with the Gospel, I do not believe.
   Seeker. Questioning, with a desire to learn more about Jesus.
   Believer. Presented with the Gospel, I chose to believe.
   Follower. Growing in faith, love, and roots. Struggling with thorns, trials, and perseverance.
   Friend. Marked by obedient love for Christ and others.
   Fisherman. Reflecting Christ and bearing fruit of righteousness and good works.

2. Where would I like to be in six months?
   Skeptic. When presented with the Gospel, I do not believe.
   Seeker. Questioning, with a desire to learn more about Jesus.
   Believer. Presented with the Gospel, I chose to believe.
   Follower. Growing in faith, love, and roots. Struggling with thorns, trials, and perseverance.
   Friend. Marked by obedient love for Christ and others.
   Fisherman. Reflecting Christ and bearing fruit of righteousness and good works.

3. What invitation do I need to respond to in order to take my next step?
   Skeptic. Repent.
   Seeker. Repent. Believe.
   Believer. Follow.
   Follower. Deny self. Pick up cross. Obey. Love Christ and others.
   Friend. Love. Obey. Go.
   Fisherman. Teach others.

4. What barriers will I face?
   Skeptic. Calloused heart, deaf ears, closed eyes.
   Seeker. Lack of clear testimony. Lack of invitation.
   Believer. Lack of root. Testing. Trouble. Persecution.
   Follower. Thorns. Worries of this life. Deceitfulness of wealth. Comfort. Self.
   Friend. Complacency. Fear. Lack of vision. Lack of equipping.
   Fisherman. Complacency. Fear. Lack of vision. Lack of equipping. Weariness.

5. What spiritual needs do I have?
   Skeptic. Prayer. Repentance. A believing friend.
   Seeker. Receive. Believe. Salvation.
   Believer. Prayer. Roots. Knowledge. Teaching. Worship. Time.
   Follower. Deny self. Trials. Endurance. Perseverance. Time. Small group relationships and
       accountability.
   Friend. Vision. Continued obedience. Equipping. Opportunity. Empowerment. Accountability
       within community.
   Fisherman. Perseverance. Faithfulness. Reliable people.

6. What steps will I take?

7. Who will I ask to hold me accountable?

Self Interview

Name   Relationship

1. What is the purpose of Christian discipleship?

2. How do you define spiritual maturity?

3. How do you measure spiritual maturity?

4. How do you measure spiritual growth?

5. Have you ever been intentionally discipled? (If so, please explain)

6. Have you ever intentionally discipled someone else? (If so, please explain)

Essential Question

What are the beliefs regarding spiritual formation among people in my circles of influence?

Learning Goal

To begin exploring the conventional beliefs about spiritual growth and maturity.

Part I. Interviews

Personal: Conduct a self-interview answering the nine interview questions. Write out your answers in the space provided in the workbook.

Peer and parent: You will interview one parent and one peer who are not a part of this class. Ask each person the interview questions. Summarize each of their answers using the interview sheets provided in the workbook.

Note: This assignment would make a great meal-time discussion with your family.

Part II. Personal Reflection

Upon completion of your interviews, read and respond to the reflection questions in the space provided in the workbook.

Reflection Question

1. Reflect on your self-interview: What did you find most interesting or surprising about your own responses to the interview questions?

2. What did you find most interesting or surprising about the interview responses that you received from the two people that you interviewed?

3. How were your interview responses similar to and/or different than the responses about what you believe impacts your attitude, actions, and behaviors on a daily basis?

   a. Identify at least two areas that were similar.

   b. Identify at least two areas that were different.

4. What questions did you discover that you struggled to answer?

5. What steps do you want to take this year to develop a fuller, more complete understanding of spiritual formation and the concepts of Christ-centered discipleship?

Part III. Assessment of Learning

Option A.   Socratic dialogue: Students will present their reflections through dialogue in small groups. Students will be graded according to the Socratic dialogue rubric.

Option B.   Presentation: Students will present their reflection paper in class. Presentations will be approximately 2-4 minutes long. Students will be graded on content, clarity, analysis, and attentiveness to other presenters.

Option C.   Paper: Write a 1-2 page reflection paper that demonstrates your interaction with the answers you received while answering the four reflection questions. Students will be graded according to the proficiency rubric for content, clarity, and analysis.

Grading Standard and Proficiency Rubric

Standard	Element not present for assessment	Does not meet standard	Meets standard at basic level	Above Average in standard
	1	2	3	4
Content	Displays no apparent understanding of the reflection questions. No details provided.	Displays a limited understanding of the reflection questions. Very few details provided. No evidence of critical thinking skills.	Displays a proficient understanding of the four reflection questions. Paper is somewhat simplistic and it appears the writer has only offered basic information to cover the requirements of the assignment. Very little evidence of critical thinking skills.	Answers the five reflection questions in a thorough and comprehensive way. The answers are backed up by significant details. Strong evidence of critical thinking.
Analysis	Provides weak or inappropriate analysis. Evidence use is irrelevant or significantly wrong.	Provides very limited analysis about the interviews. It is mostly descriptive and incomplete.	Provides adequate analysis of the interviews but is overly simplistic and does not tie together the responses in a thoughtful way.	Provides effective and in-depth analysis about the interviews. Shows excellent use of critical thinking skills. Paper is well thought-out.
Clarity	Paper is disorganized and poorly communicated, and most of the required elements are missing.	Paper is underdeveloped and simplistic, but does contain required elements of the assignment.	Paper lacks some development in its attempt to create a clear understanding of the reflection questions, but is organized and contains the required elements of the paper.	Clear, well-developed reflection paper. Communication is well organized and concise. The paper follows the format found in "How to write a one-page Bible paper."

Parent Interview

Name   Relationship

1. What is the purpose of Christian discipleship?

2. How do you define spiritual maturity?

3. How do you measure spiritual maturity?

4. How do you measure spiritual growth?

5. Have you ever been intentionally discipled? (If so, please explain)

6. Have you ever intentionally discipled someone else? (If so, please explain)

Peer Interview

Name   Relationship

1. What is the purpose of Christian discipleship?

2. How do you define spiritual maturity?

3. How do you measure spiritual maturity?

4. How do you measure spiritual growth?

5. Have you ever been intentionally discipled? (If so, please explain)

6. Have you ever intentionally discipled someone else? (If so, please explain)

Summary and Reflection

1. What did you find most interesting or surprising about your own responses?

2. What did you find most interesting or surprising about the interview responses that you received from other people?

3. How were your interview responses similar and/or different than the responses that you received from others? Identify two areas that were similar and two areas that you found different.

4. What questions do you struggle with? Explain your answer.

5. What steps do you want to take this year to develop a more complete understanding of the foundations for your own personal beliefs?

Reflect

Spiritual Formation

INVITED TO FOLLOW

Unit Essential Questions

1. What is spiritual maturity and why does it matter?

2. Why did the disciples follow Jesus and why should I follow Jesus?

Unit Learning Objectives

A. To recognize and articulate a clear, measureable understanding of God's purpose for Creation

B. To recognize and articulate a clear, measureable definition of spiritual maturity

C. To recognize and articulate a clear measureable definition of spiritual growth

D. To recognize and articulate the differences between religious and Christ-centered approaches to spiritual formation

Unit Learning Assessments

1. Reading: *Respond: Christ-Centered Discipleship*

2. Memorization: Ephesians 5:1

3. Interview Reflection Paper and Presentation

4. Graded Discussion

5. Written Reflection Assessment

Daily Essential Questions

1. How does the Bible define spiritual maturity?

2. How do I understand and apply God's design for my life? (Graded Discussion)

3. What does it mean to be with Jesus?

4. What is the cost of discipleship?

5. What is the principle of 10,000 hours?

Read through the following chapter and highlight or underline any parts that resonate with you or that that you have questions about and would like to discuss in class.

Reflect

What is the goal of spiritual formation?

It is critical to the success of any journey to identify a destination. Without a clearly understood definition of where we are going, any path we choose could be considered a correct path.

The Bible uses the word "maturity" to describe the destination of our spiritual journey.

> *"Until we all reach unity in the faith and in the knowledge of the Son of God and become mature, attaining to the whole measure of the fullness of Christ."*
> *Ephesians 4:13 (NIV)*

> *"He is the one we proclaim, admonishing and teaching everyone with all wisdom, so that we may present everyone fully mature in Christ."*
> *Colossians 1:28 (NIV)*

> *"Epaphras, who is one of you and a servant of Christ Jesus, sends greetings. He is always wrestling in prayer for you, that you may stand firm in all the will of God, mature and fully assured."*
> *Colossians 4:12 (NIV)*

What is spiritual maturity?

Initially, the idea of attempting to define spiritual maturity may seem overwhelming.

The Bible is a big book. Where do we start?

Is spiritual maturity when I finally succeed at following all the rules, or do I just have to master the Ten Commandments?

Does spiritual maturity mean that I need to make a list of all of the good things I do?

Does God keep a record of my deeds for me?

Is it enough if I just demonstrate that I am trying? Is spiritual maturity as complicated as exhibiting all the fruit of the Spirit, or is it as simple as smiling more and swearing less?

Is spiritual maturity measured by my effort and my attempts to try harder, or must I prove growth and change?

Can you relate to any of these questions?

The good news is that there are no lists and the definition is not complicated.

In fact, knowing the biblical definition of spiritual maturity is such a huge key to understanding the purpose of our life that God makes it relatively simple to discover and understand.

In order to understand where we are going, it is helpful to understand from where we have come.

To fully grasp what it means to become spiritually mature, we should begin by understanding the context of our creation.

In the very first chapter of the Bible we read:

> *"Then God said, "Let us make mankind in our image, in our likeness, so that they may rule over the fish in the sea and the birds in the sky, over the livestock and all the wild animals, and over all the creatures that move along the ground." So God created mankind in his own image, in the image of God he created them; male and female he created them."*
>
> *Genesis 1:26–27 (NIV)*

These verses are the foundation for a doctrine known as the *imago Dei*, which means "image of God."

We are created distinct from the animals to reflect the image of God.

The early church father Augustine explained the connection between the *imago Dei* and spiritual maturity by saying that you and I were created to reflect the image of God like a mirror.

Theologian John Calvin built upon Augustine's description when he suggested that prior to the entrance of sin in chapter three of Genesis, Adam and Eve were not only righteous and obedient, but they also perfectly reflected the image of God.

After Adam and Eve sinned, the image of God still remains, but it is marred and tainted by their disobedience.

Even today, as sons and daughters of Adam and Eve, the reflection of God does not cease to exist in or through our lives even if it is often unrecognizable beneath our rebellious acts of self-will and sin.

When we understand the reality of this doctrine, it helps us understand how spiritually evil people who still carry a reflection of God's image are capable of moralistic actions.

Keeping in mind the concept of the *imago Dei* and God's purpose for our lives to reflect Him and His glory, it becomes easier to identify the definition of spiritual maturity in Ephesians 5:1 where Paul writes:

"Be imitators of God."

The Greek word translated into English as "imitate" is the word "mimetes," which means "to emulate, copy, mirror, follow, model, or reflect."

What does it look like to imitate God?

To define spiritual maturity as reflecting God seems a bit broad. Inevitably, questions arise:

- What God are we meant to reflect?

- What is God like?

- What attributes of God are we supposed to reflect?

Over the years, I have observed many well-meaning individuals and groups gather around dry erase boards and easels for the purpose of discovering what it means to imitate God.

Typically, these well-intentioned groups will spend hours and sometimes even months or years creating lists of biblical characteristics like the fruit of the Spirit, the Ten Commandments, the Beatitudes, or anything else that can be quantified, like how often a person reads their Bible or attends a church service.

They do this with the goal of quantifying what it means to imitate God.

There was a group of well-intentioned men alive during the time of Jesus who attempted this very same approach to defining spiritual maturity.

But Jesus never seemed impressed with their efforts.

These men were known as the Pharisees. They were the Jewish religious leaders of the day.

They took it upon themselves to codify lists of actions from the Scriptures with the expectation that adhering their lives to their lists would please God.

But Jesus was not impressed with outward actions nor by the appearance of list keeping. Jesus was always more concerned with people's hearts.

I challenge you to find a passage in the Gospels where Jesus observes the actions of the Pharisees and says, "Wow, look at that guy. He sure does a great job keeping his list."

Search all you want in your efforts to prove me wrong, but you will not find any passages because there is nothing to find.

Making lists, and the ensuing efforts to follow, them only result in religious legalism.

This approach always ends in pride or despair.

Those of us who are good list keepers tend to feel God is lucky to have us on His team because we are so good at keeping the list we created for Him.

However, those of us who were never good at checking off lists realize before long that we can never keep the whole list. As a result, we slip into despair because we realize we can never measure up.

Another irony occurs when we realize we created such a long list that no one will be able to understand or follow it.

We begin to scale back our list, making it shorter for easier consumption by our intended audience.

However, when we start voting on what should make the final list, we become moralizers.

The minute we begin to number and prioritize our list to see what makes it and what does not, we are actually replacing God by attempting to arrive at our own definition of what it means to reflect Him.

Moralism begins with a rejection of God's sovereignty by substituting a religious system of our own creation that is designed to modify our behavior and cover our actual need for God.

Foundational to moralism is the belief that if we change our actions and get people to do the right things, then everything else will follow.

There are countless current systems of discipleship that are focused on simply getting people to obey on the outside in hopes that the heart will follow.

But in the same way that Scripture never records Jesus being impressed by the keeping of lists, the Bible also shows He was never a fan of behavior modification either.

> *"This people honors me with their lips, but their heart is far from me."*
> Matthew 15:8 (ESV)

But religious legalism and moralistic behavior modification feel and look good enough to have infiltrated many of our churches and discipleship materials.

Just check the titles of many of the popular Christian books and you will find an endless supply of resources, sermons, and assessment materials that are all based on the assumption that spiritual maturity can be achieved by trying harder, doing more of the right things, or participating in the right programs.

God does not need our help defining spiritual maturity any more than He needs our help designing another program for Him to use.

What is the solution?

Perhaps you have wondered, since God revealed His definition of spiritual maturity, then why wouldn't He also show what it looks like to reflect Him? In fact, Paul gives a picture of what spiritual maturity looks like in Ephesians 5:2.

Consider the simplicity of how Paul tells us in verse one that maturity is gained by being an imitator of God and then completes his thought in the next verse by saying:

> *"Therefore be imitators of God, as beloved children; and walk in love, just as Christ also loved you and gave himself up for us, an offering and a sacrifice to God as a fragrant aroma."*
>
> *Ephesians 5:1-2 (NASB)*

What does it look like to imitate God?

It looks like Jesus.

Not only is Paul telling us that Jesus is the model of spiritual maturity; Jesus himself said;

> *"Whoever has seen me has seen the father."*
>
> *John 14:9 (ESV)*

**Jesus is God with flesh on.
He is the perfect reflection of God.**

Throughout the New Testament, Christ is presented as the definition and perfect picture of spiritual maturity. Consider just these few instances:

> *"Until we all reach unity in the faith and in the knowledge of the Son of God and become mature, attaining to the whole measure of the fullness of Christ."*
>
> *Ephesians 4:13 (NIV)*

> *"Instead, speaking the truth in love, we will grow to become in every respect the mature body of him who is the head, that is, Christ."*
>
> *Ephesians 4:15 (NIV)*

> *"He [Christ] is the one we proclaim, admonishing and teaching everyone with all wisdom, so that we may present everyone fully mature in Christ."*
>
> *Colossians 1:28 (NIV)*

Notice the blatant connections in each of these verses between the concepts of maturity and Christ.

When we examine the full context of Ephesians 5:1-2, we see that spiritual maturity is when we reflect God just as Christ does.

Christ is our model of spiritual maturity.

Jesus Christ is not only the central figure in our salvation; He is the central figure in our spiritual growth.

Every one of the New Testament authors plainly understood that spiritual growth is the process of Christ being formed in us as we are transformed into His image.

Watch how Paul continues to clarify and highlight the centrality of Christ in our formation:

> *"My little children, for whom I labor in birth again until Christ is formed in you... I have been crucified with Christ; it is no longer I who live, but Christ lives in me."*
> *Galatians 4:19 and 2:20a (NKJV)*

> *And we all, who with unveiled faces contemplate the Lord's glory, are being transformed into his image with ever-increasing glory, which comes from the Lord, who is the Spirit.*
> *2 Corinthians 3:18 (NIV)*

When we correctly define the destination of spiritual maturity as reflecting Christ and not as the keeping of a list or attempting to modify our behavior, we realize it is not about what we do. It is about Christ being formed in us.

That is why the author of Hebrews exhorts us to fix our eyes on Jesus not only as the author but also as the finisher of our faith (Hebrews 12:1-2).

Jesus is not only our redeemer.
Jesus is our rabbi.

As believers in Christ, we often view Jesus only as a redeemer.

He is the one who gave His life in exchange for ours and rescued us from our sin and disobedient rebellion to God.

But as followers of Christ, we also need to recognize Jesus as our rabbi. He is our teacher.

He is the one who lived His life as a model for us to reflect, and He also modeled how we should reproduce His process of discipleship in the lives of others.

The Greek word in the New Testament for "disciple" is the word *mathetes*, which is from the same root for the word "reflect."

The word for disciple means, "learner or student of a master."

A disciple is an individual who learns to become a reflection of the original.

That is why in Matthew 10:24-25 Jesus states that a student will become like his teacher.

What He is really saying is that the student will be a reflection or imitator of the teacher.

It is also why those who accepted Christ's invitation were known as His followers or His disciples.

The word that was used in the original Greek is the word *mimatai*, which means, "little imitators."

When we put the pieces together, we can see the theme of reflection running through the pages of Scripture. Genesis 1:26-27 tells us we are created to reflect the image of God, and Ephesians 5:1-2 tells us we are called to reflect the image of God.

Throughout the Gospels, Jesus invites us to follow Him through the process of becoming His reflections.

When we fail to understand and embrace Christ as our rabbi, we fail to understand how Christ-centered formation takes place.

When Christ takes His rightful place as the singular focus in our quest for spiritual maturity, we move forward.

But while this clarifies and defines our ultimate destination, we must still learn how to get from where we are to where we are called to be.

In other words, if reflecting Christ is the product of discipleship, then we will next need to define the process of how discipleship works.

The next unit will help us to understand the answers to the following questions about the process of Christ being formed in us.

- If we are not to place our focus on making lists or modifying behavior, how does spiritual growth actually take place?

- Do we passively receive the new work of God in our life and hope for the best?

- Is there a specific path He has laid out for His disciples to follow that we can find through the revelation of Scripture?

Reflection

1. What are two big ideas from the article that challenged your thinking?

2. What are two questions that you have as a result of reading the article?

3. What is one idea that the article talked about that you would like to see discussed in class?

Reflection and Dialogue

- If we are not to place our focus on making lists or modifying behavior, how does spiritual growth actually take place?

- Do we passively receive the new work of God in our life and hope for the best?

- Is there a specific path He has laid out for His disciples to follow that we can find through the revelation of Scripture?

Understanding the foundation of formation

1. Check several translations and then use Ephesians 4:13 and the surrounding verses to describe spiritual maturity. In your own words.

   • Spiritual maturity is when we are not…

   • Spiritual maturity is when we are…

2. Read Genesis 1:26-27 in several different translations and then research the concept of the Imago Dei. In your own words describe the significance of the Imago Dei as it relates to the concepts of spiritual maturity.

3. Read Ephesians 5:1-2 in several different translations. Use a Bible Dictionary to do a word study on the Greek word that is translated as "reflect" or "imitate" and then compare this verse and that word with your research on the Imago Dei. In your own words describe the connection or significance between the concepts.

Understanding the foundation of formation

4. Look up the following references and identify what happened to Moses when He was in the presence of God.

    - Exodus 33:11

    - Exodus 34:29

    - Exodus 34:30

    - Exodus 34:33

5. In your own words, explain the significance of Moses' experience being in the presence of God in light of what you are discovering in the other passages.

6. Examine the following references in context and identify key words or phrases that help to define spiritual formation and maturity. Highlight or underline them in your Bible and note your reflections and insights.

    - Galatians 4:19

        "My little children, for whom I labor in birth again until Christ is formed in you…"

    - Galatians 2:20

        "I have been crucified with Christ; it is no longer I who live, but Christ lives in me…"

    - Ephesians 4:13, 15

        "Until we all reach unity in the faith and in the knowledge of the Son of God and become mature, attaining to the whole measure of the fullness of Christ." "Instead, speaking the truth in love, we will grow to become in every respect the mature body of him who is the head, that is, Christ."

    - Colossians 1:28

        "He is the one we proclaim, admonishing and teaching everyone with all wisdom, so that we may present everyone fully mature in Christ."

Understanding the foundation of formation

7. Is spiritual formation and growth an expectation for every Christian?

    Look up the following references and answer the following questions using words and phrases from within the verse(s)

    a. What is the expectation for growth that is conveyed in the text?
    b. Are there specific areas of growth that are mentioned or measured?
    c. What questions does the verse raise?

    *   Ephesians 4:14–15

    *   2 Peter 3:18

    *   Philippians 1:9

    *   1 Peter 2:2

        "We have much to say about this, but it is hard to make it clear to you because you no longer try to understand. In fact, though by this time you ought to be teachers, you need someone to teach you the elementary truths of God's word all over again. You need milk, not solid food! Anyone who lives on milk, being still an infant, is not acquainted with the teaching about righteousness. But solid food is for the mature, who by constant use have trained themselves to distinguish good from evil."

        Hebrews 5:11-14

    Observations – What are you observing from these passages?

    Applications – What do you need to apply to your life?

Understanding the foundation of formation

8. What is the significance of Jesus calling disciples to "be with" Him?

> "And he went up on the mountain and called to him those whom he desired, and they came to him. And he appointed 12 (whom he also named apostles) so that they might be with him and he might send them out to preach and have authority to cast out demons."
>
> Mark 3:13-15

In order for a disciple to become a reflection of their rabbit, the disciple needed to be with their rabbi. What did it look like for a disciple to "be with" their rabbi?

What would be the modern day equivalent of "being with" Jesus?

The Principle of 10,000 Hours

> In a study published in the Harvard Business Review in 2007, Dr. K. Anders Ericsson said excellence is not just based on practice, but *deliberate* practice. 10,000 hours to be exact.
>
> - Malcolm Gladwell, *Outliers*

Do the math ... did the Jesus model the principle of 10,000 hours with His disciples?

> Jesus invested about 6 months with His disciples through the process of inviting them to regularly spend time with Him and another 2.5 years in the context of a discipleship relationship.

Application: How long until my time with Jesus equals 10,000 hours?

A. How much time do I spend with Jesus each day?

- Each week?
- Each month?
- Each year?

B. At my current rate where will I be in ...

- 1 year?
- 5 years?
- When will I reach 10,000 hours?

Understanding the foundation of formation

9. Is it only about the time?

Explain the following statement in your own words, "It is possible to spend time with Jesus and still end up far from Him."

How would you describe the difference between Christ-centered formation and conventional formation?

10. What is Christ-centered formation?

Explain the following statement in your own words and using references from the verses that you have studied. "Ultimately, this course is not as much about spiritual formation but about Christ begin formed in us.

"He is the one we proclaim, admonishing and teaching *everyone* with all wisdom, so that we may present *everyone* fully mature in Christ."

Colossians 1:28

How do I take notes?

1.   What is the advantage of taking notes?

      Studies show that after 72 hours we normally remember:

            10% of what we _____.

            30% of what we _____.

            50% of what we _____ and _____.

            90% of what we _____, _____, and _____,

2.   Examining Acts 2:42

3.   Listen carefully to the introduction and identify three helpful tools:

      A.   What is the _____?

      B.   What is the _____?

      C.   What is the _____?

4.   Identify the main points of the outline.

Highlight and write down key points and personal application.

How do I take notes?

5.   Note questions that you

   A.   Don't _____

   B.   Don't _____

   C.   Want to _____

6.   Note sources that are mentioned and write them down to check or research later.

   A.   DO follow along in your Bible.

      (Be wary of verses that are taken out of context or misused).

         "Now the Bereans were of more noble character than the Thessalonians, for they received the message with great eagerness and examined the Scriptures every day to see if what Paul said was true."

                                                                Acts 17:11

   B.   DO NOT try to write down every word.

Application and Practice

Watch the video clips and post a response that answers at least two of the following questions. Make sure that your responses demonstrate your learning.

1.   What is your reaction to the video?

2.   What is one thing you learned?

3.   What is one thing you are still unclear about?

      Video 1. How do we know the Bible is God's Word?

      Video 2. Where did the Bible come from?

Understand

Spiritual Formation

Unit Essential Questions

1. What is the process of Christ-centered discipleship as revealed through Scripture?

2. What does it mean to "be with" Jesus?

Unit Learning Objectives

A. To understand the biblical definition of the Word of God

B. To understand the role of the Word of God in the process of discipleship

C. To examine the invitations of Jesus as they relate to the process of spiritual formation

D. To discover the spiritual needs and obstacles to growth at each stage in the process of spiritual formation

E. To understand and apply basic hermeneutical skills in the context of a word, passage, and concept study of Scripture

F. To identify and articulate the difference between biblical eisegesis and biblical exegesis

Unit Learning Assessments

1. Reading: *Respond: Christ-Centered Discipleship*

2. Memorization: Hebrews 4:12; 2 Timothy 3:16-17; 2 Timothy 2:15; 1 Corinthians 9:24-26

3. Group Projects: word study, passage study, concept study

4. Theological Reflection Project

Daily Essential Questions

1. What is the significance of rabbinical invitations?

2. What is the role of the Word of God in spiritual formation?

3. How can we study and understand the Word of God?

4. What are the invitations of Christ?

5. What are the stages of spiritual growth?

6. What are the spiritual needs and obstacles to spiritual growth?

Read through the following chapter and highlight or underline any parts that resonate with you or that that you have questions about and would like to discuss in class.

Understand

How do we know what is real?

After leaving the whiteboard and finding the definition of spiritual maturity in the pages of Scripture, it is ironic how many organizations I have worked with who return to their whiteboards with efforts to devise a plan or program that will help Christ carry out His transformational process in our lives.

But if we begin with the presupposition that as a rabbi Jesus is not only our model for what spiritual maturity looks like but He would have also modeled a process for becoming mature, then shouldn't we turn from the whiteboard and look in the Gospels to identify His process?

Bookshelves and trashcans are filled with attempts to develop plans and processes for discipleship. Each has its own language, formulas, and programs.

Sadly, we often overlook and underestimate the unpretentious invitation by Jesus to follow Him.

In context, Jesus issued His invitation from the perspective of a Jewish rabbi.

The invitation from a rabbi was a contractual offer to the prospective disciple.

The prospective disciple would not only reflect the rabbi, but he would also reproduce the methods and material of the rabbi.

It also implied an agreement that the rabbi would be responsible for the methodology and material that would be transferred to the disciple.

It is silly to think that a rabbi would invite us to follow him and then ask us to apply our own agenda.

For a disciple to follow a rabbi meant the disciple would become a reflection of that rabbi. They would agree to set aside their desires and goals for their life in order to emulate, copy, mirror, model, and reflect the life, methods and mission of their rabbi. They were to become little reflections.

Disciples of a rabbi understood they were not responsible for creating the transformational process.

Instead, they were responsible for following their rabbi, reflecting his teaching, and repeating his process of teaching with a future generation of disciples.

Reflections of Our Rabbi

As our rabbi, Jesus is not only our model for what spiritual maturity looks like; He also promises to transform us.

Jesus does not need our help or our programs. His process still works just fine.

Consider Jesus' invitation and His promise to the brothers who were fishing:

> *And He said to them, "Follow Me, and I will make you fishers of men."*
> *Matthew 4:19 (NASB)*

> *And Jesus said to them, "Follow Me, and I will make you become fishers of men."*
> *Mark 1:17 (NASB)*

Jesus promised His disciples that if they followed Him, He would transform them, and indeed He did.

One way Jesus intended that this transformation occur was through being with those He chose.

> *He appointed 12 that they might*
> *be with Him…*
>
> Mark 3:14 (NIV)

A Relationship with Our Rabbi

Jesus desired that His disciples would "be with" Him. The picture we see of the relationship between a rabbi and a disciple is one of close proximity. Discipleship is about the relationship between the rabbi and the disciple. Life-on-life contact leads to life transformation.

Mark 3:14 does not stop with the idea that Jesus wanted to simply be with His disciples in order that they might be changed. The second half of His invitation gives additional insight and purpose.

> ...*and that he might send them out to*
> *preach.*
>
> Mark 3:14 (NIV)

The transformation process in the lives of the fishermen would not be complete until those who reflected Christ reproduced His process in the lives of others. Jesus reiterates this fact in His final instructions to the disciples:

> *"…teaching them to obey everything I have*
> *commanded you."*
>
> Matthew 28:19-20 (NIV)

Jesus' call to become fishers of men is not simply for personal transformation; it is an invitation that includes the concept of duplication.

Jesus promised to not only make them His followers, but also to equip them to repeat His process in the lives of others.

In other words, Jesus is our model of spiritual maturity, and He is also our model for equipping others.

So how does this apply to our lives?

We need to embrace a larger, more accurate perspective of Jesus. Some of us have accepted Christ as our Savior and then failed to understand Him as our rabbi. We believe He died on the cross and rose from the dead, but we do not fix our eyes upon Him in every aspect of our lives. We wrongly believe we are spiritually mature if we only need and call upon Jesus during the truly critical moments of life. True spiritual maturity is not **independence** from Jesus. It comes when we recognize our complete **dependence** upon Jesus in every area of life, especially in the areas where we think we need Him least.

Consider this illustration:

If I laid a 5-foot long, two-by-four board on the floor of your house and asked you to walk across it without touching the floor, would you?

Most of us would say "yes" to this easy request.

Most of us would also accomplish this task independent of any help and with little to no effort or thought.

But consider how your response might change if I took the same board and laid it between two high-rise buildings in downtown Dubai.

Would you be willing to walk across that board if it was suspended 100 stories in the air between the tops of two skyscrapers?

The odds are that many of us would not participate.

Why?

It is the same board…
It is the same distance…
But what changed?

On the outside, all that may have changed is the height, but on the inside we may find ourselves dealing with issues of focus and trust.

Most of us have not been trained to deal with extreme heights.

Our hearts may pound. Our hands might sweat. Our focus may change from the trustworthiness of the board to the added variable of the height.

For many, this shift in focus may result in a paralyzing fear that keeps them off the board completely. For others, it might result in a misstep that could be fatal.

In spite of the fact that we would be asked to walk across the same board of the same size at the same distance, our distracted focus would lead to fear.

Focus is a critical factor in every area of life. Where we fix our eyes matters.

While I was taking a class to get my motorcycle license, one of the first lessons I learned was that the motorcycle ultimately ends up wherever the rider is focused. Wherever we fix our eyes is where the motorcycle will follow.

The same principle is true in multiple other scenarios in life, including our spiritual journey. Where we fix our eyes is where we will end up.

That is why the author of Hebrews exhorts us to fix our eyes on the One we are to reflect.

> *Fixing our eyes on Jesus, the author and perfecter of faith…*
> *Hebrews 12:2 (NASB)*

The author of Hebrews tells us Jesus is not only the perfecter of our faith (the one who is our model for maturity), but He is also the author of our faith (the one who wrote the directions for how to live the right way).

The application for you and me is that Jesus is the author of how spiritual formation takes place.

Jesus is the rabbi who invites us to become reflections of Him, and Jesus releases us to reproduce and replicate His process for reflection as we fix our eyes on Him.

These concepts of reflection and reproduction were not lost on the early church. That is why we hear the New Testament writers repeat the idea of imitation:

> *I urge you, then, be imitators of me.*
> *I Corinthians 4:16 (ESV)*

> *Be imitators of me, as I am of Christ.*
> *I Corinthians 11:1 (ESV)*

> *And you became imitators of us and of the Lord, for you received the word in much affliction, with the joy of the Holy Spirit.*
> *I Thessalonians 1:6 (ESV)*

> *So that you may not be sluggish, but imitators of those who through faith and patience inherit the promises.*
> *Hebrews 6:12 (ESV)*

In light of these verses, our job is not to design a new discipleship plan, but to discover and reproduce Christ's process for spiritual transformation.

By fixing our eyes on Jesus, we reflect Him in our lives. In this way, others see Jesus through us.

What is the role of the Word of God in the process of spiritual formation?

Notes and Discussion

What is the role of the Word of God in the process of spiritual formation?

What is the role of the Word of God in the process of spiritual formation?

What is the Word of God?

- John 1:1

- 2 Timothy 3:16

The Word of God is both _____ and _____.

How did we get the Word of God?

- The _____ Word

- The _____ Word

How does the Word of God describe itself?

- Psalm 119:105

- Psalm 119:130

- John 8:12

- John 9:5

What should my attitude be toward the Word of God?

- 2 Timothy 2:15-17

How can I understand the Word of God?

- Practice _____, not eisegesis!

- Learn to ask_____.

- Allow Scripture to _____ Scripture.

- Look at the _____.

- Practice Occam's Razor: _____.

- Don't build a doctrine around _____.

What are three effective ways to accurately study and understand the Bible?

Group Project

A Passage Study: The Parable of the Sower

- Matthew 13:1-9, 18-23

- Mark 4:3-8, 13-20

- Luke 8:5-8, 11-15

A Word Study:

- Soil

- Roots

- Rocks

- Weeds

A Concept Study: The invitations of Christ

- Repent

- Believe

- Follow

- Love/Deny

- Go/Teach

What is the role of the Word of God in the process of spiritual formation?

Notes and Discussion

Understand
Passage Study

The context for this parable is Jesus speaking first to the crowd and then directly to the disciples. Christ's use of the concept of soil to represent the hearts of the people correlates with the words of the prophet Jeremiah.

In the context of Isaiah 28:23-29, the disciples would have understood the point of Christ's parable was to examine their own hearts to assess their response to the Word of God (the seed).

The Parable of the Soils (Sower): Matthew 13:1-9, 18-23

"That same day Jesus went out of the house and sat by the lake. Such large crowds gathered around him that he got into a boat and sat in it, while all the people stood on the shore.

Then he told them many things in parables, saying: 'A farmer went out to sow his seed. As he was scattering the seed, some fell along the path, and the birds came and ate it up. Some fell on rocky places, where it did not have much soil.

It sprang up quickly, because the soil was shallow. But when the sun came up, the plants were scorched, and they withered because they had no root.

Other seed fell among thorns, which grew up and choked the plants. Still other seed fell on good soil, where it produced a crop—100, 60 or 30 times what was sown.'

'Listen then to what the parable of the sower means: When anyone hears the message about the kingdom and does not understand it, the evil one comes and snatches away what was sown in their heart.

This is the seed sown along the path. The seed falling on rocky ground refers to someone who hears the word and at once receives it with joy.

But since they have no root, they last only a short time. When trouble or persecution comes because of the word, they quickly fall away.

The seed falling among the thorns refers to someone who hears the word, but the worries of this life and the deceitfulness of wealth choke the word, making it unfruitful.

But the seed falling on good soil refers to someone who hears the word and understands it. This is the one who produces a crop, yielding 100, 60 or 30 times what was sown.'"

Understand
Passage Study

The Parable of the Soils (Sower): Mark 4:3-8, 13-20

"Listen! A farmer went out to sow his seed.

As he was scattering the seed, some fell along the path, and the birds came and ate it up.

Some fell on rocky places, where it did not have much soil. It sprang up quickly, because the soil was shallow. But when the sun came up, the plants were scorched, and they withered because they had no root.

Other seed fell among thorns, which grew up and choked the plants, so that they did not bear grain.

Still other seed fell on good soil. It came up, grew and produced a crop, some multiplying 30, some 60, some 100 times.'"

"Then Jesus said to them, 'Don't you understand this parable? How then will you understand any parable? The farmer sows the word. Some people are like seed along the path, where the word is sown. As soon as they hear it, Satan comes and takes away the word that was sown in them. Others, like seed sown on rocky places, hear the word and at once receive it with joy. But since they have no root, they last only a short time. When trouble or persecution comes because of the word, they quickly fall away.

Still others, like seed sown among thorns, hear the word; but the worries of this life, the deceitfulness of wealth and the desires for other things come in and choke the word, making it unfruitful. Others, like seed sown on good soil, hear the word, accept it, and produce a crop—some 30, some 60, some 100 times what was sown.'"

The Parable of the Soils (Sower): Luke 8:5-8, 11-15

"A farmer went out to sow his seed.

As he was scattering the seed, some fell along the path; it was trampled on, and the birds ate it up.

Some fell on rocky ground, and when it came up, the plants withered because they had no moisture.

Other seed fell among thorns, which grew up with it and choked the plants.

Still other seed fell on good soil. It came up and yielded a crop, 100 times more than was sown.'"

"This is the meaning of the parable: The seed is the word of God. Those along the path are the ones who hear, and then the devil comes and takes away the word from their hearts, so that they may not believe and be saved. Those on the rocky ground are the ones who receive the word with joy when they hear it, but they have no root. They believe for a while, but in the time of testing they fall away.

The seed that fell among thorns stands for those who hear, but as they go on their way they are choked by life's worries, riches and pleasures, and they do not mature. But the seed on good soil stands for those with a noble and good heart, who hear the word, retain it, and by persevering produce a crop.'"

The Parable of the Soils (Sower)

Observations

Who is the audience for the parable? (Hint: Check the context)

Who is the audience for the explanation of the parable?

Who is the farmer in the parable? (How do you know?)

What is the seed?

What does the ground (path/soil) represent?

What are the characteristics of:

- The path:

- The rocky places:

- The thorns:

- The good soil:

The Parable of the Soils (Sower)

Observations

What does "root" refer to in the context of the parables?

What does a person who lacks roots struggle with?

What are the rocks? (How do you know?)

What is the shallow soil? (How do you know?)

What does it mean to be scorched?

Explain the "struggle with thorns." What exactly is the struggle?

What is the difference between the plant that is scorched because they lack roots and when the seed falls among thorns?

Use the three versions of the parable to assemble a description of the "good soil." Beyond the crop that the good soil produces, what sets the good soil apart?

Soil	Path	Shallow	Weeds	Fruit Bearing
What are the characteristics of each stage?				
What needs to exist at each stage?				
What obstacles to growth exist at each stage?				
What is a general description of each stage?				

What is the role of the Word of God in the process of spiritual formation?

Context study

67

What is the role of the Word of God in the process of spiritual formation?

Word Study

What are the invitations of Christ?

- Repent

- Believe

- Follow

- Love

- Deny

- Go

- Teach

What is the role of the Word of God in the process of spiritual formation?

Word Study
Project Template

What are the invitations of Christ?

Invitation	References	Version	Context	Cross Reference (Is it the same or a different time in each Gospel?)	Description of the person or group being spoken to.	Response of the person or group being spoken to.
Repent						
Believe						
Follow						
Love						
Deny						
Go						
Teach						

Reflection

1. What are three of the most thought provoking ideas or "a ha" moments from your studies so far?

   A.

   B.

   C.

2. What is one thing that you would like to keep studying on your own?

What is the role of the Word of God in the process of spiritual formation?

Putting the pieces together

Define assessment.

How did Christ assess hearts?

Define differentiation.

How did Christ differentiate His teaching based on His assessment?

What is the application for spiritual formation?

Theological Reflection Project

1. Outline the invitations of Christ.

    - What are they?
    - How do you know?
    - Give examples.

2. Profile the stages of spiritual growth.

    Use references to provide descriptions of each stage. Include:

    A. The invitations of Christ

    B. The barriers or obstacles to growth at each stage

    C. Spiritual growth needs

3. What additional insights from your word study did you learn?

4. Give a personal reflection on the process of Christ-centered spiritual growth and transformation.

Repent

Spiritual Formation

INVITED TO FOLLOW

Unit Essential Questions

1. How does Christ's invitation to repent apply to my life?

2. Where are the areas in my life that I need to change my mind about Jesus?

Unit Learning Objectives

A. To understand the invitation to repent from the perspective of Christ-centered formation

B. To identify and articulate the concept of the fullness of Christ

C. To examine and discuss in community the person of Christ as revealed in the book of Colossians

D. To reflect on my personal perspective of the incarnation of Christ and how my perspective impacts my daily life

Unit Learning Assessments

1. Reading: *Respond: Christ-Centered Discipleship*
   Colossians

2. Memorization: John 1:14

3. Socratic Dialogue: Colossians Journal and Community Discussion

4. Incarnation Perspective Project

Daily Essential Questions

1. Why did Jesus invite people to repent?

2. What does it mean to repent? Small Group Activity

3. What is the fullness of Christ?

4. How do my beliefs impact my perspective of Jesus?

5. How is Jesus revealed in Colossians?

6. Assessment: What is my perspective of Christ?

Read through the following chapter and highlight or underline any parts that resonate with you or that that you have questions about and would like to discuss in class.

Repent
What is the meaning of the invitation to repent?

A recent study of over 45,000 Christian high school students from countries on six continents revealed that 9 out of 10 students consider themselves to be Christians, and 7 out of 10 desire to live a life worthy of Jesus Christ.[1]

At first, those numbers may sound very positive, but the students in the study also admit that less than 1 out of every 2 are actually getting to know Jesus by investing in time with Him on a regular basis.

The addition of the second set of numbers paints a picture of an average Christian high school student whose heart may be in the right place but whose understanding of who Jesus truly is may not be accurate.

The Corinthian church spoken of in the Bible struggled with a similar scenario where, in spite of their good intentions, they were in danger of misunderstanding who Jesus truly was.

It was in this context that the Apostle Paul wrote them these words:

> *"I am afraid that just as Eve was deceived by the serpent's cunning, your minds may somehow be led astray from your sincere and pure devotion to Christ.*
>
> *For if someone comes to you and preaches a Jesus other than the Jesus we preached, or if you receive a different spirit from the Spirit you received, or a different Gospel from the one you accepted, you put up with it easily enough. "*
>
> *2 Corinthians 11:3-4 (NIV)*

Our contemporary culture presents a lot of different images of Jesus.

- There are versions of Jesus wearing sandals and flashing a peace sign.

- Other variations have Jesus on the back of a motorcycle.

- While still others prefer to envision a Jesus who would be driving a tank.

More often than not, the version of Jesus that modern culture presents is either a really nice guy who helped people by saying really nice things or an irrelevant extremist who was potentially misunderstood.

Our culture is not a lot different than the culture at the time of Christ. There were many different perspectives and expectations of the Messiah during His generation too.

Christ lived at a time when there were many teachers who attracted crowds by declaring themselves to be the messiah of the Jewish people.

However, their definition was of a political messiah and their promise was to relieve the people of Roman occupation and rule.

The Gospels reveal that Jesus spent much of His two and a half years of ministry urging people to change their minds about who they thought He was and who they wanted Him to be.

His invitation to change their minds began with His invitation to repent.

The word "repent" means,
"to change your mind."

Jesus' first use of the word "repent" was immediately after the beheading of John the Baptist.

> *"After John was put in prison, Jesus went into Galilee, proclaiming the good news of God. 'The time has come,' he said. 'The kingdom of God has come near. Repent and believe the good news!'"*
>
> *Mark 1:14-15 (NIV)*

When Jesus gives the invitation to repent, He is inviting us to change our minds about who we think He is and how we relate to Him. In other words, He is God and we are not.

In addition to changing our mind, repentance is also the process of relinquishing our desire to be God or to take the place of God in any area of our life.

* Repentance is evident at the point of salvation when we recognize that we cannot "save ourselves," but that it is only by receiving the gift of God's work through Christ's death and resurrection that we can be forgiven and made right with God.

It is good news when we embrace this change of mind. However, the Gospels also record some of Jesus' harshest words for those who failed to change their minds about Him in spite of the evidence they were given.

> *"Then Jesus began to denounce the towns in which most of his miracles had been performed, because they did not repent."*
>
> *Matthew 11:20 (NIV)*

> *"Woe to you, Chorazin! Woe to you, Bethsaida! For if the miracles that were performed in you had been performed in Tyre and Sidon, they would have repented long ago in sackcloth and ashes."*
>
> *Matthew 11:21, Luke 10:13 (NIV)*

Reflection. What do you think?

Is repentance only for those whose hearts are hard and skeptical toward Christ, or is it something that those who have received the gift of salvation need to revisit?

Revisiting Repentance

Too often followers of Christ view repentance as a one-time thing.

Too often we view repentance as a part of the Christian life that is in the rearview mirror.

We look back on it as the thing we did at the moment of our salvation.

We see it as the invitation we accepted when we admitted we were sinners who could not get to heaven on our own merits.

It was the moment in time that we repented and were justified before God.

For some of us, repentance felt kind of like taking a bath or a quick shower: a cleansing.

Confronted with the enormity of our sin and the consequences brought upon us by our rebellion against God, we repented.

We recognized our inability to save ourselves. We changed our minds about Jesus, made Him our Savior, and then, having cleaned up, we moved on.

The concept of repentance is not only foundational in our relationship with Christ, it is not something that is a single occurrence; it is something that we must revisit frequently as we continually renew our mind to reflect Christ in every area.

But a "one and done" approach to repentance is not what Jesus meant when He exhorted,

"Produce fruit in keeping with repentance."
Matthew 3:8 (NIV)

Repentance is an ongoing process that continues after our initial moment of salvation as we continue to renew our mind and become imitators of Christ in every area of our lives (Romans 12:1-2, 2 Corinthians 10:5).

If we look in the New Testament book of Revelation, we discover that the act of repentance, or changing our mind about Christ, is continual and not just a one-time act.

"Consider how far you have fallen! Repent and do the things you did at first. If you do not repent, I will come to you and remove your lampstand from its place."
Revelation 2:5 (NIV)

"Remember, therefore, what you have received and heard; hold it fast, and repent. But if you do not wake up, I will come like a thief, and you will not know at what time I will come to you."
Revelation 3:3 (NIV)

"Those whom I love I rebuke and discipline. So be earnest and repent."
Revelation 3:19 (NIV)

Do Not Misunderstand

The Bible is clear that our justification and salvation is a one-time deal.

We do not need to make the error of continuously recommitting our lives to Christ in an effort to renew our eternal fire insurance policy or maintain our salvation. Repeating an act of salvation through *"recommitment ceremonies"* is not biblical.

But a lifestyle of continuous, transformative repentance that brings us back to the cross and continuously renews our minds about Christ is part of our process of sanctification.

It is part of the process of taking every thought captive and renewing our minds until every part of our lives is a reflection of Christ.

God's Grace Leads to Repentance

When I was 14, I rode my yellow, 10-speed bike everywhere. Looking back on some of the places that I rode and their distance from my house is both shocking and impressive.

As a 14-year-old in an age before cell phones, it never dawned on me to give a second thought to riding hours from home. In retrospect, my lack of good judgment should have impacted me a lot more than it did because there were times when I found myself 20 miles from home.

It was not uncommon for me to spend a lot of time riding with my hands off the handlebars. I would either rest them on my knees in order to sit upright and stretch my back or hold them out like a bird, away from my body to enjoy the breeze.

One day, I wanted to see how far I could ride without touching the handlebars. I remember being fairly impressed with myself.

So much so, that, as I approached the last couple of blocks from my house, a thought crossed my mind: I should see if I could continue to ride with no hands down and around the long, sweeping corner that led to my house at the bottom of the hill. After all, I was a pretty good bike rider.

What was the worst that could happen?

My hands went to my knees and the bike picked up speed. Fighting the temptation to reach forward and apply the brakes, my momentum increased until I found myself barreling down the hill at a terrifying rate.

As I neared the bottom of the hill, my bike began to quiver. I learned I had overestimated my abilities.

At that moment, I repented.

I changed my mind and reached for the brakes, but it was too late.

Rain had washed loose sand and gravel down the hill and it had accumulated at the bottom. Attempting to brake on this surface at that velocity caused my bike to wipe out. I slid down the rest of the hill atop the loose gravel, which embedded itself into my legs.

The shock of not making it all the way to the bottom, coupled with the embarrassment of foolishly thinking I could, was dull in comparison to the pain of the emergency room visit and the treatment that followed for the next several weeks. The gravel was so deeply embedded that all of it could not be removed in one session.

The emergency room doctors made their best effort to pick out all the gravel they could. After that, their directive to me was to use a hard-bristled scrub brush every day for the next several weeks to continue getting as much gravel out of my leg as possible.

Eventually my body would follow a natural process of identifying the gravel as foreign and pushing it to the surface. Rubbing the bristles of the scrub brush over the area removed a little more gravel each day.

Repentance acts like the scrub brush in our relationship with Christ.

The Holy Spirit of God graciously brings things to the surface of our lives and gives us the opportunity to remove them by responding to Christ's invitation to change our minds, to repent.

In our first act of repentance, we recognize our inability to save ourselves, but that is not the only false belief we hold about Christ. As we assent to His other invitations to believe in Him, to follow Him, to love Him, and to deny our selfish desires, we begin to recognize additional foreign values and thoughts that need to come to the surface to be removed from our lives.

In many ways, it is God's grace that repentance is a continuous act rather than a one-time surgery. He recognizes that much of our self-dependence is deeply embedded. He must carefully and lovingly bring it to the surface in order to help us continually reflect Him in every way.

Changing our mind about Christ is about embracing a fuller vision of God. God does not change, but our understanding of Him does.

As we begin to understand more about who God is and we recognize areas in our life where we are still attempting to usurp His authority, we repent.

As we change our minds, hearts, attitudes, and actions follow, because repentance includes inviting God to replace our desires with His.

- Repentance is about acknowledging our false beliefs that we can be self-sufficient and that we have the independent power to change ourselves while operating under our own will and authority.

- Repentance is about asking: Who or what do I really worship with my life? What are the idols that keep me from God?

- Repentance is about examining and discovering what or who is at the center of our time, talent, and treasure, as well as changing our minds about what our life is centered upon.

Recognize that all of this is the exact opposite of Adam and Eve's actions in the Garden of Eden when they deliberately rebelled against the authority of God. They chose to place their desire to become "like God" over the fact that He was and is God, and they were not.

This desire led them to embrace a false image of themselves. They viewed their relationship with God, not from the perspective that the created serve their Creator, but as they wanted it to be, with God existing to submit to their desires and will.

The Lord invites us to view Him as He really is, not as we want Him to be from our self-centered, self-serving desires for Him.

This idea was one of the major problems that those who initially heard Christ's invitation to repent struggled with. They were looking for a political messiah to come in and rescue them from the Roman occupiers.

They wanted someone like Moses, who freed Israel from slavery in Egypt. They wanted someone like Joshua or one of the ancient Israelite judges who were willing to lead an army and raise a sword to take what they believed was rightfully theirs.

They did not desire a Messiah who would die on a cross to free them from their captivity to the law and their slavery to their own sins.

They wanted a messiah who would meet their felt needs and accomplish their desires for political freedom.

Jesus invited them to change their understanding of who He was and is and the type of true, eternal freedom He brought.

Consider the tense exchange in John 8 as Jesus again attempts to bring the religious leaders to a mind change about who He is.

"Jesus replied, 'Very truly I tell you, everyone who sins is a slave to sin. Now a slave has no permanent place in the family, but a son belongs to it forever. So if the Son sets you free, you will be free indeed. I know that you are Abraham's descendants. Yet you are looking for a way to kill me, because you have no room for my word.'"

John 8:34-37

Christ is speaking to a group of religious leaders known as the Pharisees in this passage. The Pharisees believed that if they followed the law religiously (even to the point of adding to it), their own righteous living would cause God to act and the Messiah would come to deliver Israel from their oppressors.

The result would not only be the removal of the oppressive Roman rule over their land, but the re-establishment of the unrivaled blessing of God based on the promise of God through Moses in the book of Deuteronomy.

The Pharisees struggled to accept His claim to be their Messiah because in their minds if He was indeed the Messiah, why did He not praise them for their righteous acts? Why did He not set them free from Roman rule?

Consider for a moment how often we relate to Jesus in a similar way. Have you ever found yourself thinking you deserve something from God because of the nice things you have done? Have you ever approached a day, a test, or even a trial in your life with the thought, "I've been good in the morning, so hopefully God owes me something good in return in the afternoon?"

I doubt that is has ever been that blatant, but I think we all fall victim to this mentality. Perhaps it is more like, "I don't get it. Why aren't things working out for me? I play by all the rules, I work really hard, I do what I'm told, and I still don't have what I want."

Have you ever experienced the feeling that rises up within us that we deserve better? When we operate in this manner, we are no different than the Pharisees who believed that the Messiah would arrive in response to their good works to meet their needs and fulfill their agenda.

The irony is that this process of thinking and approaching God on our terms is typically very subtle and can be relatively undetectable.

Often it is buried deep within our hearts and disguised under what often appears to be a very moral lifestyle.

Ironically, when we approach God with our own expectations and on our own terms, He will inevitably fail to meet our expectations just like He did for the Pharisees.

The resulting emotions from failed expectations will often manifest themselves in the form of confusion, disappointment, regret, and anger. Left unchecked, each of these have the propensity to lead to bitterness and the desire for retaliation.

Consider how things progressed for the Pharisees when Jesus failed to meet their improper expectations and desires for their messiah. Eventually their disappointment led to a deep seeded anger and a form of bitterness that resulted in His death.

Their bitterness from Christ not meeting their misplaced expectations led them to miss the grace of God that was right in front of them.

The same is eventually true in our lives when we approach God with false expectations based on our own misplaced understanding of who He truly is.

Eventually this "false Jesus" is destined to disappoint us, and when he does, we are prone to respond in ways similarly to the Pharisees.

Have you ever heard someone talk about how they "tried God, but it just didn't work for them?" Or how they could never "believe in a God who did…"

Often these words are indicators of a heart reeling from unmet expectations. The sad truth beneath the words is that, like the Pharisees, the unmet expectations from a false perspective of God resulted in a painful bitterness that resulted in the death of God in their lives.

The author of Hebrews references the idea that bitterness in our hearts is like a deep-rooted weed that causes us to miss the grace of God (Hebrews 12:15).

This bitterness that causes us to miss God's grace and results in further separation from God is why the invitation of repentance is so foundational to our process of transformation.

By changing our mind about who we think God is and understand Him to be, we literally exchange our way of thinking for His way of thinking. And to do that often means the hard work of examining our lives, our thoughts, and the motives of our hearts.

Our way of thinking places us at the center of our lives. His way of thinking has Him at the center of everything.

Our way of thinking places our will above His will.

Our way of thinking believes that we can handle our own sin, problems, trials, and temptations. His way of thinking informs us that only He is sufficient to handle every aspect of our lives, and that apart from Him we can do nothing (John 5:15).

Our way of thinking leads us down the road toward religious attempts to do good works and modify behavior through personal willpower.

His way of thinking invites us to walk in the work He has already accomplished under the power of the Holy Spirit.

Our way of thinking is centered on ourselves. God's way invites us to center our lives on Christ.

The process of repentance is not easy. It is not the mumbling of a few words or a moment in time after a spiritual life week or camp-like experience.

Repentance is not a quick shower to wash off our sin. It is more like the removal of the rocks, weeds, and roots that have become embedded in our hearts. Repentance is the turning over of the soil of our hearts to receive the Word of God.

Repentance kills the weeds that attack our hearts.

A few years ago, my family moved into a new house. Well, it was new to us at least. It is an older home that had been through foreclosure. As a result, it needed a lot of repair.

One of the things that hadn't been kept up was the lawn.

We bought the house in the winter, when there was still snow. It was not until after we closed the purchase that I saw we had more weeds than grass surrounding our house. The situation was bad.

It was impossible to walk or play in the yard without shoes. There were a couple of weeds in particular that had become so deeply rooted they were now the size of small trees. They were impossible to pull out because the roots were so deep.

After a weekend of trying to address the issues, my wife and I realized that the problem was beyond our abilities.

We needed professional help.

Rueben

After searching for a lawn care specialist, Rueben arrived to give me an estimate for what it would take and how much it would cost to remove the weeds, stickers, and dandelions that plagued my lawn. Immediately, it became obvious that Reuben was not just a professional, but an expert with many long years of experience restoring lawns like ours.

Reuben told me not to pull up the weeds. Doing so risks fixing the surface only temporarily while the root would still exist.

The key was to allow Reuben to treat them with a weed killer that would attack the root. This action would address the real issue and not just what could be seen on the surface.

The temptation of viewing religious behavior as a way to modify our sin is like pulling weeds. Things may look good temporarily, but we have failed to remove the root.

When we fall into the temptation of religion and attempt to modify our behavior through self-will and effort, we address only surface issues.

While others may be initially impressed by our work, we still miss the opportunity repentance brings to remove the root of the sin.

While I may temporarily improve my actions, my willpower cannot hold me back when I am tried or have a bad day. Without removing the root, I am destined to return to my previous poor patterns of behavior and thought because the root remains.

Will power is not self sustaining. We can only get so far under our own power. Our will also has a tendency toward fantasy, not reality. This is why so many people fail to keep new years resolutions to eat healthy, exercise more, or break addictions.

Take a look through the window of your local health club at the beginning of January and then again at the end of January and you will see evidence of our inability to turn our good desires and intentions into lasting change.

This is why the empowerment of the Holy Spirit is so crucial in process of transformation.

The Principle of Time

Fixing my lawn did not happen overnight. Some of the weeds were so deeply rooted that they needed to be hit two or even three times.

Sometimes we want God to magically and mystically remove the weeds in our hearts and minds instantaneously without any effort on our part.

When we demand that He remove our sin and its consequences so that it does not trouble our lives anymore, it is still a self centered, rather than a Christ-centered, prayer. Our focus is typically on our own comfort and how we will feel when the painful sin has been removed or how we will benefit from our perceived good choice.

But this focus on self preservation or comfort is rooted in an approaching God as if He exists to serve us and meet our needs.

Like the Pharisees, we miss the grace that is directly in front of us because God desires for us to be closer to Him through the humbling process of transformation in ways that quick fixes do not always allow.

Repentance is designed to bring us to the point of humility before God. It is when we recognize that He is God and we are not that His Spirit is finally able to work in and through our lives. It is this process of continual repentance and renewal that we change our mind about both Him and ourselves.

It is through this process of realizing our limitations that He increases and we decrease.

Yet, the irony and the tension in the process of transformation is that, while it is a process that must be entirely powered by the Spirit of God, it is not a process that relinquishes us from the responsibility of full participation.

This can be seen clearly in God's instructions through Moses to the people of Israel as they were preparing to cross the Jordan River and enter into the land that God had promised to them.

'Although the Lord your God has given you this land as your property, all your fighting men must cross the Jordan ahead of your Israelite relatives, armed and ready to assist them.

Deuteronomy 3:18b

Do you see the tension? God has "given" them the land as "their property," but "all" their fighting men must cross the river "armed and ready."

Perhaps nowhere is this tension between God's part and our part more pronounced than in His instructions to Joshua prior to the fall of Jericho in Joshua 6:2-3.

As people looked upon the gates of Jericho God says to Joshua, "I have given you Jericho, it's king, and all its strong warriors. You and your fighting men should march around the town once a day for six days."

Now, few would dare to argue that when the walls collapsed on the seventh day that it was not a complete miracle that could only be credited to God. Yet, God still invited the people to participate by doing the work of walking in faith for a week.

God wants us to understand that we are insufficient alone, and He must be truly sufficient in everything in order for us to walk in true freedom.

But, God also wants us involved in the process of learning to walk in dependence upon Him as He reforms our spirits to reflect Him.

Without Him, we can't; without us, He won't.

God's goal is not simply to remove the blight of sin and offer salvation or a better life.

His goal is to remove the root of self reliance, self preservation, and self glorification in order for us to truly embrace and experience a Christ-centered life.

Check out how Paul speaks to this concept:

"Put to death, therefore, whatever belongs to your earthly nature: sexual immorality, impurity, lust, evil desires and greed, which is idolatry. Because of these, the wrath of God is coming. You used to walk in these ways, in the life you once lived. But now you must also rid yourselves of all such things as these: anger, rage, malice, slander, and filthy language from your lips. Do not lie to each other, since you have taken off your old self with its practices and have put on the new self, which is being renewed in knowledge in the image of its Creator. "

Colossians 3:5-10 (NIV)

The weeds in my lawn are gone, but there are still a lot of roots underneath the dirt and mulch in my flowerbeds. Reuben warned me that they are there, and he told me to be quick to hit them with weed killer as soon as they appear.

There are also still some bare spots on my lawn, but this fall we plan on seeding. By next spring, we hope to see the results of the work being done this year. Right now, we have a plan, and the lawn is in the process of being sanctified.

Our lives are the same way.

We need to be quick to return to the invitation of repentance every time the Spirit of God reveals a new weed, and we must not allow it to take root in our lives. We need to seed our hearts with the Word of God to continue to identify misbeliefs and misperceptions about how we view our Lord and ourselves.

Repentance Is What Leads us to Embrace the Fullness of Christ

Repentance is more than a mere assent to a statement of facts.

It is a true changing of our hearts in response to the truth. Without the truth of God's Word continually seeding our hearts, there can be no true repentance because there cannot be an accurate transforming of the mind.

Every time my intentions, thoughts, or actions are not a clear reflection of Christ, my mind needs to be renewed.

"We demolish arguments and every pretension that sets itself up against the knowledge of God, and we take captive every thought to make it obedient to Christ."

2 Corinthians 10:5 (NIV)

"Therefore, I urge you, brothers and sisters, in view of God's mercy, to offer your bodies as a living sacrifice, holy and pleasing to God—this is your true and proper worship.

Do not conform to the pattern of this world, but be transformed by the renewing of your mind. Then you will be able to test and approve what God's will is—his good, pleasing and perfect will."

Romans 12:1-2 (NIV)

The fruit of repentance may be change in our outward behavior, but the root of repentance begins with an internal understanding and honest admission of our present state in order to respond and embrace the truth through the renewing of our mind.

Without truth, there can be no grace. Grace without truth is not a reflection of God's love any more than truth without grace offers a full reflection.

If there is no true objective standard or understanding of our broken state, then there is no true objective measure of grace that can be applied to it.

If there is no grace to apply to our broken state, then we are abandoned and orphaned; designed to be stuck in our sinfulness.

Grace is always a gift, not an obligation. We cannot earn God's grace; He bestows it upon us freely out of love. If it was given out of obligation, it would not be a gift.

The Game of Life

When my children were little, we used to play The Game of Life™.

It is a board game that involves driving a little car with tiny pegs that represent people around a game board.

Players react to cards with instructions dictating what type of job or how many kids they have.

The goal of the game is to reach retirement with the most money and possessions.

The game epitomizes the materialistic worldview: the individual who arrives at the end of the game of life with the most stuff wins.

It is a game based on consumerism that poses the question:

What can I get out of life?

But Christ presents Himself as the way to real life, and He informs us that it is through Him that we may have "life to the full."

> *"Jesus answered, 'I am the way and the truth and the life. No one comes to the Father except through me.' "*
>
> *John 14:6 (NIV)*

> *"The thief comes only to steal and kill and destroy; I have come that they may have life, and have it to the full."*
>
> *John 10:10 (NIV)*

The Game of Life™ subtly instills in us that in order to have a happy life, we need more stuff.

More money will buy more toys and ultimately, more happiness.

Christ claims that more of Him and less of ourselves will lead to a life of peace, joy, and satisfaction.

To be truly satisfied in life, we must look to the "I Am" and find ourselves in Christ.

In order to move from a conventional view of life to a Christ-centered view, we need to change our minds. We need to repent.

The message the world repeats through marketing jingles sells us products that bring temporary self-satisfaction and even occasional happiness.

In contrast, Christ invites us to find ourselves, our lives, our hope, and our satisfaction in Him alone. He wants us to find our forgiveness in Him, and He wants us to find our ability to forgive others through Him.

- He desires to replace the counsel of the world with the counsel of His Word.

- He desires to replace the insecurity of our functional saviors with the security of His Son.

- He desires for us to stop caring about how others perceive us and allow Him to replace our need for self with a desire for Him. Christ desires to change our minds so that He can change the motivation of our hearts.

True repentance begins when we reflect Christ's example and care about the will of His Father in the same manner He did.

> *"For whoever does the will of my Father in heaven is my brother and sister and mother."*
>
> *Matthew 12:50 (NIV)*

> *"Jesus said to them, 'My food is to do the will of him who sent me and to accomplish his work.' "*
>
> *John 4:34 (ESV)*

Ultimately, the model set by Christ and the path He invites us to follow is exemplified in His response to the Father's will in the Garden of Gethsemane.

He placed the will of God the Father over His own desire to avert the pain of the Cross and embraced the Father's will for the sake of our redemption.

We see and hear His example through His prayer,

"Father, if You are willing, remove this cup from Me; yet not My will, but Yours be done"
Luke 22:42

Christ's prayer illustrates the life He invites us to imitate.

A life where we follow in His steps by taking every thought, action, and attitude of our heart and place it before the Father with the words, "Not my will, but yours be done."

This is the move from self-centered living to Christ-centered living that can only occur after we begin to change our minds about who Christ is and how we relate to Him.

How Does God Lead People to Repentance?

On State Street in downtown Chicago, there used to be a man with a milk crate, a few signs, and a bullhorn who would stand on the street corner and boldly proclaim his message to those who passed by.

His message was repentance.

His words told of an impending judgement from God and that those who refused to turn from their sin would burn in Hell.

My guess is that he viewed himself as a modern day prophet. Perhaps he saw himself as a modern day John the Baptist, a voice crying out in the wilderness of downtown Chicago.

However, my personal feeling, is that it is possible his reflection was less like John the Baptist and closer to that of the clanging cymbal that Paul references in 1 Corinthians 13.

Listening to him made me wonder:

- Are the tactics of this street preacher the same tactics God uses to lead us to repentance?

- Does God yell at us with a bullhorn?

- Did Jesus yell at people to "turn or burn?"

According to Paul, it is the love and gentleness of God, not a bullhorn like tactic, that leads us to repentance.

"Or do you show contempt for the riches of his kindness, forbearance and patience, not realizing that God's kindness is intended to lead you to repentance?"
Romans 2:4 (NIV)

In his second letter to Timothy he writes about how gentleness will lead people to repentance.

"Opponents must be gently instructed, in the hope that God will grant them repentance leading them to a knowledge of the truth."

2 Timothy 2:25 (NIV)

Examine your life.

Where have you seen or experienced the kindness and gentleness of God inviting or leading you toward repentance and a more accurate knowledge of Him?

Where are the times when God has gently been revealing Himself to you?

It is His desire that you would be brought to a full understanding of the truth about who you are and who He is.

How will you respond to the invitation to repent?

Citation
1. The 2013 Global Student Assessment. WheatonPress.com

Individual Exercise
Part I. Understanding the invitation to repent.

According to Hebrews 6:1, in the process of spiritual formation, what level of teaching is repentance considered to be?

What does it literally mean to repent of something?

Word study

Look up the following verses and use them to define the word *repent*. Look for repeated words or key phrases in each of the verses and then put them together to form a definition.

- 1 Kings 8:47

- 2 Chronicles 6:37

- 2 Chronicles 32:26

- Job 34:33

- Ezekiel 14:6

Write a practical definition of repentance using words from the verses that you have studied.

Individual Exercise
Part II. Understanding the invitation to repent.

Explain the statement, "True change means that we not only turn *from* something but *to* something."

Passage study

At the core of the invitation to repent is the invitation to change our hearts and our minds about where we are placing our trust. When we place our trust in something or someone other than Jesus, that thing or person becomes a false god (or an idol) in our life.

According to Revelation 9:20-21, what are some of the false gods that we are tempted to place our trust in and are invited to change our minds and hearts about? (Note: There are at least 10).

1.

2.

3.

4.

5.

6.

7.

8.

9.

10.

Personal Reflection
Part III. Understanding the invitation to repent.

What do we turn from?

The word *worship* literally means "worth-ship" and it carries with it the concept of ascribing worth to something. In other words, when we worship Jesus, what we are really saying is that we believe Jesus is "worthy" of our trust, focus, hope, and praise. We are saying that we trust Him to save us.

In Revelation 9:20-21, the word "worship" is used to imply that people put their faith in the things that they consider to save them and/or what they treat as gods in their lives.

Take some personal reflection—what do you find yourself putting your faith in or treating as a god in your life? Why?

What are you giving worth too? Where is your focus, time, trust, etc.?

What do we turn to?

In Acts 20:21, Paul specifically directs people to turn to something or someone.
Who or what are they to turn to and what is the specific action they are to take?

A. What does it say? (Use the words of the text to describe what is being said).

B. What does it mean? (Use your words to describe what is meant).

Small Group Exercise
Part IV. Understanding the invitation to repent.

According to the following verses, what does God do in order to lead people to repentance?

Step 1. What does it say?
Look up each verse and using the words from the verse or passage, summarize your answer in the space provided.

Step 2. What does it mean?
Read over the verse summaries and then summarize your answer in the space provided.

A. What does it say?

- Romans 2:4

- 2 Corinthians 7:9

- 2 Corinthians 7:10

- 2 Timothy 2:25

- 2 Peter 3:9

- Revelation 2:21

B. What does it mean?

Small Group Exercise
Part V. Understanding the invitation to repent.

According to the following verses, what is God's attitude and promise to those who need to repent?

Look up each verse and use the words from the text to summarize what each verse says, then in the space at the bottom explain what it means.

A. What does it say?

- Jeremiah 18:8

- Ezekiel 18:32

- Luke 17:3-4

B. What does it mean?

Part VI. What is the result of true repentance?

What did Jesus mean when He said that we are to "produce fruit in keeping with repentance"?
(Matthew 3:8)

Look up the following verses and identify the fruit of repentance, then summarize the answers to formulate an understandable explanation of what Jesus meant.

A. What does it say?

- Jeremiah 31:19

- Zechariah 1:6

- Acts 26:20

- Revelation 16:9

B. What does it mean?

C. What is the underlying principle regarding the fruit of repentance?

Small Group Exercise

Part VII. Changing our minds about Jesus.

Context study

According to the following verses, what was Jesus inviting people to change their minds about?

Look at the verses in context and identify who Jesus was talking to and what He was specifically inviting a person to change their minds about.

A. What does it say?

- Matthew 3:2

- Mark 1:15

- Matthew 4:17

B. What does it mean?

Part VIII. Connecting and applying

Jesus invited people to "Repent, for the kingdom of heaven is at hand."
Based on the following verses; what was Jesus referring to as the kingdom of heaven?

A. What does it say?

- Luke 24:27

- Acts 2:38

- Acts 3:19

- Acts 11:18

B. What does it mean?

Large Group Reflection
Participating in the mission of God

What does it all mean?

What is the fullness of Christ?

"Until we all attain to the unity of the faith and of the knowledge of the Son of God, to mature manhood, to the measure of the stature of the fullness of Christ."

Ephesians 4:13

What is the fullness of Christ?

Notes and Discussion

What is my perspective of the incarnation and what are the implications of incomplete views of Christ?

Essential Question

How is my perspective on the fullness of Christ impacting my reflection of Jesus?

Learning Goal

To articulate understanding and application of the concept of the fullness of Christ

Part I. Reflection paper

Purpose: The student will use this paper to demonstrate an understanding of the concepts and application of the incarnational view of Christ in their life.

Directions: Write a 1-2 page reflection paper that demonstrates your understanding of the concepts behind the incarnational view of Christ and answers the four questions below using the guidelines for a one-page paper.
- Do you most easily identify with Jesus from the perspective of truth, glory or grace? (Demonstrate your understanding of why.)
- How might this be affecting your relationship with Jesus? (Use your answer to demonstrate your understanding of the concepts involved.)
- What perspective are you lacking?
- What steps can you (and will you) take to develop a fuller, more complete understanding of the person and work of Jesus?

Students will demonstrate understanding of the following concepts as articulated through the assigned reading and the classroom lectures:

The Ministry of Jesus Christ as truth, grace, and glory:

A. Jesus = Truth
- His ministry is to proclaim the Word of God
- Jesus not only proclaimed the written Word of God, but was literally the incarnate living Word of God.

B. Jesus = Grace
- His ministry is to mediate between God and man
- Jesus is the superior high priest
- Jesus is the superior sacrifice
- Jesus is the superior intercessor

C. Jesus = Glory
- His ministry is to rule over all material and immaterial worlds
- Jesus revealed His glory through His death on the cross

Part II. Presentation

Directions: Students will present their reflection paper in class. Presentations will be approximately 2-4 minutes long. Students will be graded on content, preparedness, attentiveness to other presenters, and how well the presentation articulates an understanding of the concepts.

Believe

Spiritual Formation

INVITED TO FOLLOW

Unit Essential Questions

1. How does Christ's invitation to believe apply to every area of my life?

2. Where are the areas in my life that I need to invite God to help me believe?

Unit Learning Objectives

A. To identify, examine and explain the elements of the gospel

B. To examine the tension between doubt, trust, and belief

C. To examine and dialogue about the tension between grace and legalism found in Galatians

D. To dialogue exegetically in the context of various small and large groups

Unit Learning Assessments

1. Reading: *Respond: Christ-Centered Discipleship*
   Galatians

2. Memorization: John 3:16-17; 1 Corinthians 15:1-6

3. Socratic Dialogue: Galatians Journal and Community Discussion

4. Gospel Elements Assessment

Daily Essential Questions

1. Why did Jesus invite people to believe?

2. What is the gospel?

3. What is the tension between discipleship and religion in Galatians 1-3?

4. What are the consequences of belief in Galatians 4-6?

5. How does what I believe impact how I live?

6. What does a mature follower of Christ believe?

Read through the following chapter and highlight or underline any parts that resonate with you or that that you have questions about and would like to discuss in class.

Believe

What is the meaning of the invitation to believe?

Jesus invites those who were skeptical about Him to repent and change their minds, but for those who were seeking Him in earnest, He would couple His invitation for a change of mind with an invitation for a change of heart.

> *"'The time has come,' he said. 'The kingdom of God has come near. Repent and believe the good news!'"*
>
> *Mark 1:15 (NIV)*

Are these two invitations marked by two distinct actions, or are they one and the same?

Here is an easy way to mark the similarities and the distinctions between the invitations to repent and believe.

- To repent is to change our mind and to turn away from our own ideas and our own will.

- To believe is to change our heart and to place our faith in God's ideas and His will. It is not enough to simply replace our ideas and our will they must match His.

We can see the relationship and the distinction between belief and faith in Paul's words to the believers in Rome.

> *If you declare with your mouth, "Jesus is Lord," and believe in your heart that God raised him from the dead, you will be saved.*
>
> *Romans 10:9 (NIV)*

So what does this mean, and how does it apply?

Belief Is the Activity that Accompanies Repentance

- Repentance is turning away from faith in our self.

- Belief is actively turning toward Christ in faith.

Both are as much a reflection of the attitude of our heart as they are of our posture.

The Desire of Our Hearts

The Hebrew word for this is the word *kavanah*, which means, "the intention or true desire of our hearts."

The word *kavanah* means more than which direction our heart faces. It also carries connotations of being bent.

Kavanah is the direction towards which the heart is bent.

To understand the significance of *kavanah* in relationship to belief, it is helpful to understand the Shema.

The Shema

In the time of Christ, it was the duty of every Jew to recite the Shema.

> *Hear, O Israel: The LORD our God, the LORD is one. Love the LORD your God with all your heart and with all your soul and with all your strength.*
>
> *These commandments that I give you today are to be on your hearts. Impress them on your children. Talk about them when you sit at home and when you walk along the road, when you lie down and when you get up.*
>
> *Tie them as symbols on your hands and bind them on your foreheads. Write them on the doorframes of your houses and on your gates.*
>
> *Deuteronomy 6:4-9 (NIV)*

Jewish religious leaders teach that it is not enough to just recite the Shema or to go through the motions of obedience.

The recitation is to be connected to the direction of the heart.

The word that they use is *kavanah*.

To consider it another way, our words must not only recognize the lordship of Christ in our lives, but our hearts must be directed or "bent" toward Him as well.

The word *kavanah* is a verb; it implies action.

Belief is a verb.

By its very nature, belief implies more than intellectual consent. It is a reflection of the position of our heart based on reasoned hope.

The result of reasoned faith and belief is confidence that something is true and reliable.

It is only when our beliefs are grounded deeply in the reliability of God's truth that we can act with purpose, meaning, and direction.

Without reasoned belief, we are left to falter, stumble, and ultimately go astray or suffer with questions about our direction and ourselves.

Reasoned Belief Leads to Conviction

To believe means we are fully persuaded in the reliability of a thing. Belief is not stagnant, and identifying and changing our false beliefs does not happen without intentionality.

Every time God invites us to believe His truth, it is to replace a lie from His enemy.

We live in a world that has conditioned us to think, act, and feel a certain way.

Survival of the fittest is the religion of biology class. "God helps those who help themselves," is a saying that is not found anywhere in the Bible, yet holds the title of one of the most well-known "Bible passages."[1]

One of the foundational understandings of faith is that our daily actions are reflections of our core beliefs.

Every belief we have that is not based on a truth of God is a lie.

Accepting Christ's invitation to believe is the process of learning to identify lies that are in opposition to the truth of Christ.

Identification occurs through the revelation of the Word of God.

Deserting the Truth

In Galatians, we learn how quickly the people of God can turn from truth and embrace lies, even under the guise of religious piety.

Paul is quick to address this action with some fairly strong language:

"I am astonished that you are so quickly deserting the one who called you to live in the grace of Christ and are turning to a different gospel—which is really no gospel at all. Evidently some people are throwing you into confusion and are trying to pervert the gospel of Christ. But even if we or an angel from heaven should preach a gospel other than the one we preached to you, let them be under God's curse! As we have already said, so now I say again: If anybody is preaching to you a gospel other than what you accepted, let them be under God's curse!"

Galatians 1:6-9 (NIV)

How often do our lives reflect the lives of the Galatians rather than the life of Christ?

As we turn away from the truth of God's Word, we learn to trust ourselves, our methods, our process, our programs.

Rather than responding to the invitations of Christ and following His path, we make our own path and invite God to bless it.

When was the last time you paused to study God's Word with the intention of examining your beliefs about God for accuracy?

What is God inviting you to believe about Him?

Where is He asking you to stop placing your faith in yourself and begin placing your faith in Him?

Spiritually Scorched

In Christ's Parable of the Soils, He describes the spiritual heart condition of individuals who are motivated and who seem to grow rapidly, but in whose hearts, the soil is rocky. Because they lack spiritual roots, they quickly become scorched.

If you have ever seen something completely scorched by the sun, it is not a pretty sight.

Scorching occurs when a plant's water supply is completely dried up. The plant dies. Even when no life remains, the heat of the sun will cause it to continue to wither until what was once a vibrant plant literally turns to dust.

How can we avoid becoming spiritually scorched?

Paul helps us understand the answer as he returns to Christ's concepts of our need for spiritual roots when he equates the concept of spiritual roots with knowledge.

> *Rooted and built up in him, strengthened in the faith as you were taught, and overflowing with thankfulness.*
> Colossians 2:7 (NIV)

Without spiritual roots, our hearts may be in the right place, but we are still at risk of uninformed intentions leading us astray.

Time and time again, I've watched well-intentioned people buy into a version of Christianity that is based on emotion that leads them to ride cycles of spiritual highs and lows like a roller coaster at a theme park.

The problem is that Satan understands that when the emotion dries up, there is often very little left to sustain the well-intentioned believer.

After the adrenaline rush is gone and exhaustion sets in, the temptation is to seek another emotional high in a manner similar to a drug user pursuing another, "better" high.

Or, some will push Christianity away, and say, "I tried it, but it did not work for me."

Mature faith and belief occur when we commit all we know about ourselves to all we know about God.

However, when what we know about God is shallow understanding, assumed conjecture, or false truth, we risk being scorched. While we may receive the word of God with joy, if we have no roots, the results can be devastating.

"Those on the rocky ground are the ones who receive the word with joy when they hear it, but they have no root. They believe for a while, but in the time of testing they fall away."

Luke 8:13 (NIV)

Burnt Over

This pattern of seeking highs can be seen through the historical movements known as the First and Second Great Awakenings.

This period was marked by people who would seek an emotional high without stopping to be rooted or grounded in the knowledge and understanding of spiritual truth.

So widespread was the desire for an emotion-based spiritual high, an area of the country in upstate New York came to be known as "The Burned Over District" because "the flames of revival" had burned over the area so many times.

The result was a season of hellfire-and-brimstone preaching that is still studied in American schools to this day.

What is often missed in our education of the time period is that it was also a time of great "awakenings" for new cults and false religions.

People were susceptible to unbiblical teaching because they were focused on emotion; they lacked spiritual roots of knowledge and discernment of the truth the Bible actually teaches.

A partial list of some of the cults that came into being at this time can also be found in the book, *Respond: Christ-Centered Discipleship.*

Just a handful of these groups include:

- The Mormons, who teach that Jesus is the half-brother of Lucifer.

- The Millerites, who preached that Christ would return on October 22, 1844.

- The Fox sisters, who started the American Spiritualism movement and practiced séances and communion with the dead.

- The Shakers, who were known for some unique beliefs and practices. For example, Shakers believed that God is both male and female. Anyone who joined their community was expected to remain celibate. In addition, they believed that Jesus was the male manifestation of Christ, and that Mother Ann, who was the daughter of an English blacksmith, was the female version of the Incarnation.

- Last, but certainly not least, the Oneida Society, which believed in free love and group marriage to the point that exclusive sexual relationships were frowned upon as being too possessive.

The irony is that each of these claimed (or still claim) to be followers of Jesus.

But in comparison with the Jesus of the Bible, what Jesus were they following?

The issues for those who follow one of these non-biblical versions of Jesus is not a lack of sincerity, but a lack of knowledge of the truth.

Certainly they were, or are, very sincere.

But sincerity does not make something true.

The Gap Between Sincerity and Ignorance

Paul addresses the problems that arise when there is a gap between sincerity and ignorance in his second letter to the church in Corinth.

> "But I am afraid that just as Eve was deceived by the serpent's cunning, your minds may somehow be led astray from your sincere and pure devotion to Christ. For if someone comes to you and preaches a Jesus other than the Jesus we preached, or if you receive a different spirit from the Spirit you received, or a different gospel from the one you accepted, you put up with it easily enough."
> 2 Corinthians 11:3-4 (NIV)

History confirms Scripture by informing us that it is easy to be sincere and still stray off the path.

While some of these false teachings have died out, others are gaining traction and are still finding new converts who accept and believe their anti-biblical teaching about Christ.

**The result is that people
are still being scorched.**

Without roots, we are in danger of following our good intentions and becoming scorched by false teaching.

Check Your Motivation

We also place ourselves in peril when our motivation for attending church is based on a desire to "feel better" or to get an emotional lift as opposed to an act of worship with the intention of renewing our mind under the authority of God's Word.

This attitude puts us at risk of treating God like a mood-altering drug that we seek out for an occasional high when we are feeling down or depressed.

A person with a drug habit can sometimes be referred to as a "user." We are at risk of approaching God from the perspective of a drug addicted "user" when our focus is about God existing to meet our needs and make our lives more tolerable.

This self-centered approach of using God to meet our needs is the opposite of what Paul wrote when he described the life that is pleasing to God.

> "Therefore, I urge you, brothers and sisters, in view of God's mercy, to offer your bodies as a living sacrifice, holy and pleasing to God—this is your true and proper worship."
> Romans 12:1 (NIV)

The life that pleases God is centered on Christ, not on ourselves.

Recognizing the Roller Coaster

The stage of spiritual growth where we move from believer to follower presents us with a lot of new information inviting us to renew our minds and replace self-centered lies with Christ-centered truth.

> Having our minds challenged to think differently is difficult.

At times it may feel overwhelming.

It is easy to view lots of informative knowledge as unnecessary. We love Jesus; shouldn't that be enough?

But at this stage in our spiritual growth, our head is just as much at risk as our hearts.

It was this concern that caused Paul to tell the Corinthian church that he feared for them.

Reading his letter feels eerily prophetic of what occurred amongst the well-intentioned revivalists in early America whose minds were deceived by the false gospels of so many upstart cults.

To make it past this stage of growth without getting scorched, we need to recognize that feelings will not last, nor do they determine truth.

Otherwise, we end up riding a roller coaster of feelings and emotions. The spiritual highs lead me to believe God is good and He loves me. But when the spiritual highs go away, our feelings will lead us to believe that God has left us and no longer cares.

None of this focus on our need for knowledge is intended to nullify our human emotions. Jesus was fully human, and He experienced the breadth of human emotions. But to make it past this stage of growth without getting scorched, we need to recognize that feelings change.

To grow spiritual roots that will last, we must formulate not only what we believe, but also why we believe, as the Bible commands us to know.

Peter exhorts us to have a faith that is reasonable and not based on hype or emotion. He describes a reasonable faith as one in which we can articulate or explain the reason for the hope that is within us.

> *"But in your hearts revere Christ as Lord. Always be prepared to give an answer to everyone who asks you to give the reason for the hope that you have. But do this with gentleness and respect."*
>
> *1 Peter 3:15 (NIV)*

The Christianity of the Bible is not a system of fantasy where followers "check their brains at the door" and participate in actions of conviction based on blind faith with little or no evidence.

On the contrary, core to Christ's teaching is His command to love the Lord God "with all your mind" (Matthew 22:37, Mark 12:30, Luke 10:27).

Rooted and Established

Roots help us formulate not only what we believe, but also whether or not it is reasonable to believe.

One of the wonderful things about following Christ is that we are invited to examine our faith.

We are invited to love the Lord our God with all of our heart, soul, strength, and mind (Deuteronomy 6:4-9).

Belief and faith are not consistent with fantasy.

That is what makes the foundations of a rooted and reasoned faith so important.

If we build upon a shaky foundation, no matter how wonderful everything feels or looks on the outside, it is bound to give way under the stress of testing.

This concept is what Jesus references in the Parable of the Soils.

It is why He finishes His Sermon on the Mount by saying it is the wise man who hears His words and chooses to dig down and build his house upon the rock (Matthew 7:24).

In the illustration, Jesus points out that many people choose to avoid the difficult work of laying a solid foundation and, as a result, end up with an unexamined life based on the false beliefs and incomplete perspectives of reality that eventually have the effect of shifting sand during the storms of life.

God invites us to a reasoned life of examined beliefs and reasoned faith.

Unexamined beliefs lead to unreasoned faith that often manifests itself through uncertainty and insecurity.

Lost

As a person who is directionally challenged, yet who loves to travel and explore, it is easy to find myself lost in new environments.

What initially feels like an exciting, unplanned adventure over the open road can quickly become something different after the sun sets and my gas tank begins to approach empty.

Without an idea of where I am or where the nearest gas station might be, my mind will begin replaying my previous failures like a movie in my head. And with every minute, I can sense my confidence sagging and my insecurity rising.

Lack of knowledge has a way of increasing insecurity and decreasing confidence.

When we are assured in our beliefs, we will act with confidence.

Because Our Beliefs Determine Our Actions

A lack of security in our beliefs also leads to uncertainty in our interactions with others.

When we have not examined our beliefs, we may vocally echo what we have been told to believe while our actions hypocritically give a different voice to what our hearts truly believe.

The axiom that our actions speak louder than words rings true because words carry little meaning when contradicted by our actions.

When the storms of life blow, our unexamined and unarticulated beliefs reveal that our foundation has been built upon sand and will not last (Matthew 7:26).

Perhaps acts of hypocrisy reflect inner turmoil and the insecurity of an unexamined life.

In light of this image, we should pity people who struggle with hypocrisy, rather than judge them.

Doubt is not a sin.

But unaddressed doubt is like a cancer to a foundation of belief.

Addressing our doubts and solidifying our reasons for belief is the focus of the next section.

Citation

1. Mohler, Albert. "The Scandal of Biblical Illiteracy: It's Our Problem." Christianity.com.
   http://www.christianity.com/1270946/

Believe

Notes and Discussion

"For God so loved the world that he gave his one and only Son, that whoever believes in him shall not perish but have eternal life. For God did not send his Son into the world to condemn the world, but to save the world through him."

John 3:16-17 (NIV)

"For God so loved the world, that he gave his only Son, that whoever believes in him should not perish but have eternal life. For God did not send his Son into the world to condemn the world, but in order that the world might be saved through him."

John 3:16-17 (ESV)

Memory Verse Study

Examine the full chapter and answer the question, how does this passage give further context to the definition of the gospel?

Verse overview:

Passage study:

Concept study:

"Now, brothers, I want to remind you of the gospel I preached to you, which you received and on which you have taken your stand. By this gospel you are saved, if you hold firmly to the word I preached to you. Otherwise, you have believed in vain.
For what I received I passed on to you as of first importance: that Christ died for our sins according to the Scriptures, that he was buried, that he was raised on the third day according to the Scriptures, and that he appeared to Peter, and then to the Twelve. After that, he appeared to more than 500 of the brothers at the same time, most of whom are still living, though some have fallen asleep."
1 Corinthians 15:1-6 (NIV)

"Now I would remind you, brothers, of the gospel I preached to you, which you received, in which you stand, and by which you are being saved, if you hold fast to the word I preached to you—unless you believed in vain. For I delivered to you as of first importance what I also received: that Christ died for our sins in accordance with the Scriptures, that he was buried, that he was raised on the third day in accordance with the Scriptures, and that he appeared to Peter, then to the Twelve. Then he appeared to more than 500 brothers at one time, most of whom are still alive, though some have fallen asleep."
1 Corinthians 15:1-6 (ESV)

Memory Verse Study

According to Paul's description in 1 Corinthians 15, what are the elements of the gospel? What is the impact and the application of these verses beyond personal salvation?

How does this passage further define the gospel when corroborated with the previous study on "belief" in John 3?

Follow

Spiritual Formation

INVITED TO FOLLOW

Unit Essential Questions

1. How does Christ's invitation to follow Him apply to my life?

2. Where are the areas in my life that I need to be more intentional about following Jesus, and what steps do I need to take?

Unit Learning Objectives

A. To understand that following Jesus is a relationship that occurs through the grace and power of the Holy Spirit

B. To understand and articulate the difference between belief and followership

C. To understand and articulate the role and purpose of the basic spiritual disciplines

D. To examine the tension between doubt and belief in the context of community dialogue

Unit Learning Assessments

1. Reading: *Respond: Christ-Centered Discipleship*
   2 Peter, 1 John

2. Memorization: Romans 12:1-2, Colossians 2:6-10

3. Socratic Dialogue: 2 Peter, 1 John Journal and Community Discussion

4. Personal Spiritual Growth Project

Daily Essential Questions

1. What is the Mentor Project?

2. What is the difference between believers and followers of Jesus?

3. How did Jesus disciple those who followed Him?

4. How do we recognize false teachers?

5. What is the role of spiritual disciplines in discipleship?

6. How do I embrace grace and connect to the power of the Holy Spirit?

Introduction to the Mentor Project
Assignment Guidelines

Purpose

This assignment gives you an opportunity to get to know an older, more mature believer. This person should be someone who will (and perhaps already has) set an example for you in your faith and can be a source of wisdom, encouragement, and accountability. They will also be able to provide help in areas where you are struggling with temptation and sin. Additionally, this assignment gives you an opportunity to practice being accountable to someone else, a practice many believers throughout the centuries have found highly valuable in their spiritual lives, as they have experienced growth through vulnerability and authentic relationships.

- You will meet with your mentor four times in the next eight weeks.
- You will be given guidelines for each meeting (in the following pages of this packet).
- You will turn in a typed, one-page journal entry after each of your meetings. Guidelines for each journal entry will be included below.

Choosing a Mentor

> "Remember your leaders, those who spoke to you the word of God. Consider the outcome of their way of life, and imitate their faith. Jesus Christ is the same yesterday, today and forever."
>
> Hebrews 13:7

Some things to consider when choosing a mentor:

1. Who do you know who reflects Christ most clearly to you?
2. Who is a mature leader in your life that you want to imitate?
3. Does this person demonstrate an active and growing faith in God?
4. Is this someone who has characteristics I want to see developed in my own life?
5. Is this someone who would be an encouragement to me?
6. Is this someone I feel comfortable around, and with whom I'm really able to be myself?
7. Can I be honest with this person?
8. Will I be able to receive help and correction from them in areas where I need it?

You must identify your mentor THIS WEEK. Start early! If your first choice doesn't work out, you will need to find another option.

Mentor Partner Responsibilities

- You will meet with a student four times over the next eight weeks.
- Each meeting will have a specific theme and question to help guide the discussion and focus. These students will be answering this question and reflecting on their meetings with you in a journal that is due after each meeting.

Read through the following chapter and highlight or underline any parts that resonate with you or that that you have questions about and would like to discuss in class.

Follow

What is the meaning of the invitation to follow?

Learning to Hear His Voice

A surprisingly large part of Christ's Sermon on the Mount contains warnings to His listeners about false teaching and false teachers. Followers of Christ at every stage must continually guard their minds against unorthodox teaching, but Jesus pulls no punches when He warns those new to His teaching that they must be on their guard.

It was important to Jesus that those wishing to build their lives upon the rock of His teaching know that false teachers not only exist, but are potentially and often difficult to detect.

The danger of being misled is so important that Jesus put this information front and center in His Sermon on the Mount.

> *"Watch out for false prophets. They come to you in sheep's clothing, but inwardly they are ferocious wolves."*
>
> *Matthew 7:15 (NIV)*

In a similar manner, both Paul and Peter are quick to admonish and exhort their listeners to be on guard as well. In Acts, we read Luke's account of Paul's dramatic warning to the church in Ephesus to be wary of those he referred to as savage wolves.

> *I know that after I leave, savage wolves will come in among you and will not spare the flock. Even from your own number men will arise and distort the truth in order to draw away disciples after them. So be on your guard! Remember that for three years I never stopped warning each of you night and day with tears.*
>
> *Acts 20:29-31 (NIV)*

Similar warnings to be on guard against the cunning of false teachers masquerading within the walls of the church can be found in Ephesians, I Corinthians, I Timothy and 2 Peter.

> *"Then we will no longer be infants, tossed back and forth by the waves, and blown here and there by every wind of teaching and by the cunning and craftiness of people in their deceitful scheming."*
>
> *Ephesians 4:14 (NIV)*

> *"Be on your guard; stand firm in the faith; be courageous; be strong."*
>
> *I Corinthians 16:13 (NIV)*

> *"Timothy, guard what has been entrusted to your care. Turn away from godless chatter and the opposing ideas of what is falsely called knowledge, which some have professed and in so doing have departed from the faith."*
>
> *I Timothy 6:20-21 (NIV)*

> *"He writes the same way in all his letters, speaking in them of these matters. His letters contain some things that are hard to understand, which ignorant and unstable people distort, as they do the other Scriptures, to their own destruction.*
>
> *Therefore, dear friends, since you have been forewarned, be on your guard so that you may not be carried away by the error of the lawless and fall from your secure position."*
>
> *2 Peter 3:16-17 (NIV)*

The contrast to reaping the consequence brought about by following the direction of false teachers or those with uninformed, though good intentions, is to learn to take every thought captive until our thoughts reflect Christ's.

> "In your relationships with one another, have the same mindset as Christ Jesus."
> Philippians 2:5 (NIV)

> "We demolish arguments and every pretension that sets itself up against the knowledge of God, and we take captive every thought to make it obedient to Christ."
> 2 Corinthians 10:5 (NIV)

In light of the reality of false teachers, we need to do more than read the Bible or blindly accept a teaching simply because it has become popular. We need to study it for ourselves to become familiar with the truth. This is part of the invitation to believe.

When Paul and Barnabas traveled from Thessaloniki to Berea they found a group of eager and engaged people who examined the Scriptures against the teaching of the apostles for themselves.

Luke records in Acts 17 that instead of being rebuffed, they were considered noble and instead of resulting in skepticism, their study resulted in belief.

> Now these were more noble-minded than those in Thessalonica, for they received the word with great eagerness, examining the Scriptures daily to see whether these things were so. Therefore many of them believed, along with a number of prominent Greek women and men.
> Acts 17:11-12

In a generation where faith is being redefined as fantasy, and biblical illiteracy is on the rise, it is not enough for us to hold to a simple goal of simply "holding onto" or "not losing" our faith.

We live in a generation that demands that you are able to defend, articulate and communicate your faith with gentleness and respect and with reason.

We need to receive and apply Paul's admonitions to the young Timothy who found himself in a similar situation in a similar generation where he was wrestling with false teachers invading the church of Ephesus while also protecting those around him who were vulnerable to false teaching.

To Timothy, Paul writes these admonitions;

> "Watch your life and doctrine closely. Persevere in them, because if you do, you will save both yourself and your hearers."
> 1 Timothy 4:16 (NIV)

> "Study to show yourself approved by God, a workman who need not be ashamed, rightly dividing the word of truth."
> 2 Timothy 2:15 (MEV)

> "For the time will come when people will not put up with sound doctrine. Instead, to suit their own desires, they will gather around them a great number of teachers to say what their itching ears want to hear."
> 2 Timothy 4:3 (NIV)

It is only through continuous, renewed study and application of God's Word through the power of The Holy Spirit that we can come face to face with God's revelation.

To be deeply rooted in the truth we need to discipline ourselves to read, study and apply the truth of God to our lives

We do not read God's Word to earn His favor.

We do not read God's Word to increase or maintain our salvation.

We do not read God's Word to perform a religious activity.

We read God's Word to personalize our relationship with Him by gaining an accurate understanding of ourselves and our relational God.

It is only when we are rooted in truth that we can withstand the wiles of our enemy and the storms of life. (Ephesians 6:11, Matthew 7:24-27).

The Transforming Power of Truth

> Digging deep into the Word of God leads to understanding.
>
> Understanding leads to fruit.
>
> Fruit builds confidence.
>
> But it takes time, energy, intentionality, and effort.

Paul writes:

> *"Therefore I do not run like someone running aimlessly; I do not fight like a boxer beating the air."*
>
> *I Corinthians 9:26 (NIV)*

Study and discipline take time, but they pay rich rewards.

They are what separate the well-intentioned from the firmly rooted.

In John's Gospel, he uses the words "belief" and "faith" interchangeably. In the book of John, Jesus compares belief to work:

> *"Then they asked him, 'What must we do to do the works God requires?' Jesus answered, 'The work of God is this: to believe in the one he has sent.' "*
>
> *John 6:28-29 (NIV)*

Sometimes we are too quick to try to skim a verse like this one only to miss a word like "work." Too often belief is perceived as something that is passive. The idea that Christ invites us to the work of belief seems foreign.

The Work of Faith

Whether directly or indirectly, many of us have accepted a false notion that belief does not involve work. We have bought into the unbiblical concept that belief is something that simply happens from the gift of God without the act of faith. In so doing, we have accepted the idea that faith and ignorance are synonymous. Perhaps we have been told that Jesus did all the work and that we are the beneficiaries who simply need to check our brains at the door and agree to a "blind faith."

True faith involves work.

Remember the wise man had to dig deep into rock in order to lay a foundation that was firm. It was the man with the sandcastle who avoided work.

The Activity of Faith

Without nullifying or diminishing the grace of God, Jesus describes faith as bold determination.

Bold perseverance.
Bold initiative.

Time and again, Jesus recognizes active faith and commends individuals for it.

To the Samaritan leper, Jesus said, *"Your faith has made you well."*

> *Luke 17:19 (NIV)*

To the woman who anointed His feet with her tears and wiped them with her hair, Jesus said, *"Your faith has saved you" (Luke 7:50 NIV).*

In both of those instances, as well as in the cases of the woman who had the issue of blood in Luke 8:48, and the group who took the initiative of dropping their friend through the roof of a crowded house in Luke 5:19, Jesus commented on and recognized bold, active faith in them, and countless others:

> *"Then Jesus said to her, 'Woman, you have great faith! Your request is granted." And her daughter was healed at that moment."'*
> *Matthew 15:28 (NIV)*

> *"Jesus said to him, 'Receive your sight; your faith has healed you."'*
> *Luke 18:42 (NIV)*

> *"'Go,' said Jesus, 'your faith has healed you." Immediately he received his sight and followed Jesus along the road."'*
> *Mark 10:52 (NIV)*

It is this same bold, active, and determined faith that Jesus spoke of when He told the story of the woman and the unjust judge (Luke 18:1-8).

It is this boldness Paul had in mind when he wrote that he kneels with confidence before the throne (Ephesians 3:14-19).

The fruit of this active, bold belief and the outcome of reasoned faith is confidence.

The apostles who were with Jesus and who personally connected with Him after the resurrection were known for their boldness.

1. Ask yourself, "is my life marked by Spirit filled confidence in my relationship with Christ?" Why or why not?

2. Would the people who know me recognize that I have been with Jesus? How?

3. Other than the fact that as a Christian I get to spend eternity in the presence of God how is my life marked as different because I have a relationship with Jesus?

3. Am I unflinching like the apostles or am I timid like Peter in the garden prior to the cross? Why?

Paul wrote of this issue to Timothy, warning him against tentative living in the face of attack.

> *"For the Spirit God gave us does not make us timid, but gives us power, love and self-discipline."*
> *2 Timothy 1:7 (NIV)*

Weak faith lacks persistence.

Maturing faith perseveres in the face of remarkable odds.

The 11th chapter of Hebrews is filled with the names of those from the Old Testament who experienced and exercised mature, confident faith in the face of insurmountable odds.

Sincerity Is Not Enough

Our faith must be fixed upon actual truth.
We must fight the temptation to confuse sincerity with truth.

Faith is only reasonable when it is grounded in truth. No matter how much I believe that I have the skills or talents to become a rocket scientist or basketball all-star, these are fantasies. They are fun to chase, but not realistic to trust.

Belief does not make something true.

Sincerity of belief does not make something trustworthy.

What makes Christ and His teaching true is not our belief in Him, but rather, the fact that He is the embodiment and personification of truth itself (John 1:14).

That is where we derive our confidence.

That is why Jesus invites us to test Him for falsehood and to examine His claims to see if they withstand the test.

> *"Can any of you prove me guilty of sin? If I am telling the truth, why don't you believe me?"*
>
> *John 8:46 (NIV)*

He desires us to place our confidence in Him so our roots can be established, and we can stand firm throughout the storms of life.

But what about those times when we doubt?

Isn't doubt still a reality for even the staunchest believer? After all, just prior to his death, even John the Baptist wrestled with doubt (Luke 7:19).

Our Struggle with Doubt

In chapter nine of the book of Mark, Jesus comes down from the mountain where He was transfigured before Peter, James, and John.

There He finds His disciples, a large crowd, and a collection of teachers of the law arguing. A distraught father explains to Jesus that his son had been robbed of speech and had been possessed by a demon since childhood. The father had brought his son to the disciples, but they could not free him.

As you read the story, you can hear the grief in the voice of the father as he describes the demonic oppression of his son. The demon had been causing his boy to foam at the mouth and gnash his teeth. It had caused him to convulse and had thrown him into water and even into fire for the purpose of ending his life.

Jesus was his last hope.

The father brought the boy to Jesus with the belief that Christ was the only hope for his boy to be normal.

Scripture does not tell us how long the man traveled or about the conversation at home prior to the decision to take the boy to Jesus.

No doubt it was an act of desperation.

Perhaps Jesus, who had helped others in similar circumstances, could help him. So, he approached the disciples first, and then he found himself face to face with Jesus.

So he asked.

> *"If you can do anything, take pity on us and help us."*
>
> *Mark 9:22 (NIV)*

And Jesus responded with a statement that seems to challenge the man's belief.

"Everything is possible for one who believes."

Out of options, it is easy to see the man's predicament. Most likely he had placed his faith in doctors and others who had claimed healing powers (divine or otherwise) in the past only to be disappointed.

He could have attempted to lie to Christ and claim a rock solid belief in His power to heal. But instead he chooses the courageous route of simple honesty.

"Immediately the boy's father exclaimed, 'I do believe; help me overcome my unbelief!'"
Mark 9:23-24 (NIV)

What is so awesome about this moment is the total lack of pretense from the boy's father toward Christ?

The boy's father has absolutely nothing to hide and nothing to lose. His reaction is a mix of pure honesty and sheer desperation.

In my opinion, it is truly one of the greatest prayers recorded in Scripture because there is no pretense.

Too often we try to hide our feelings, struggles, and doubts from God under the false pretense that either He is unaware of them, or that we have the potential to impress Him. It is silly to think we can conceal our struggles from God.

The Bible tells us that God knows every hair on our head; certainly He knows the thoughts and anxiousness of our hearts.

So, why do we sometimes feel the need to put on a show for God?

Remember, God is not impressed by our outward behavior or actions; He is concerned with our hearts. Instead of trying to fool or impress God, shouldn't we follow the example of a man that Scripture refers to as someone who chased after the heart of God?

David

"Search me, God, and know my heart; test me and know my anxious thoughts."
Psalm 139:23 (NIV)

David, the Israelite king in the Old Testament was called a man after God's own heart, and openly voiced his struggles and doubts throughout his writings in the Psalms.

Again and again, Scripture records how David returned to steadfast trust in the goodness of the Lord. Yet, God never punished him in his moments of doubt and weakness. God never slandered him or made fun of him for his honesty in communicating his doubts and struggles.

Elijah

The Old Testament prophet Elijah is another man who grappled through tough emotions and with his desire for God to save him from the hands of his enemies.

Elijah's story demonstrates how even one of the strongest prophets of God could deal with a crisis of belief on a personal level.

You may already be familiar with Elijah's story in 1 Kings 17-19 during the reign of King Ahab. As a punishment for the sins of the king and the people, God told Elijah that rain in the land would stop until God gave His permission again. In any agrarian culture that depends upon crops for food and for livelihood, this occurrence is a big deal.

If you are familiar with the landscape and geography of Israel, you know that this punishment could have a major effect on the land. Without rain to fill the Jordan, it does not take long before Israel turns into a large bowl of dust.

Three years passed, during which God miraculously sustained Elijah until God directed him to return to Ahab and his evil wife, Jezebel, for a confrontation on the top of Mount Carmel.

It was there that God empowered Elijah to face over 400 idolatrous prophets in a showdown that culminated in fire from heaven and the slaughter of hundreds of false prophets who had been leading people away from God into various perversions.

But, the story of the miraculous power and sustaining work of God through Elijah's life gets even better.

Not only does God send fire from heaven and remove the evil priest and prophets, He also sent rain to release the people from the famine.

After a time of private prayer, Elijah returns to his servant with a message from God that rain was coming. So much rain, in fact, that he tells King Ahab to make a run for it while there is still time (1 Kings 18:45).

To call Elijah's story a mountaintop faith experience seems poetically appropriate.

But what happened next is perhaps as comforting as it is shocking.

An already exhausted Elijah runs down the mountain away from the impending storm at such a high speed that he outruns the kings fastest horses until he is finally a safe distance away, only to have his life threatened by the evil queen Jezebel.

Leaving his servant, he fears for his life, runs further into the wilderness alone, and then collapses under a broom tree and utters the words, "I have had enough, Lord…Take my life; I am no better than my ancestors"
(1 Kings 19:4 NIV).

It would be easy to judge Elijah in a negative way.

After all, from what he had seen the past three years, shouldn't he have been above any type of struggle, fear, or doubt?

Comforting Words

While we do not revel in his pain, it is natural to find a level of consolation in the truth noted by James that,

> *"Elijah was a person just like us."*
> James 5:17 (CEB)

Perhaps even more comforting is that instead of chastising him for his struggle, God mercifully meets him in his time of need by giving him food and rest from his journey.

Belief is not something we check off our list of spiritual activities on our road to maturity. Like repentance, it is an invitation from God we continually revisit.

Unbelief Is Not Something Passively Conquered

Rather, it is something we must diligently confront in our journey to change our minds and place our faith in Christ in every area of our lives.

This is where Christ's invitation to follow matters. Following Christ is the transformative process of sanctification at work in our hearts and minds as we leave doubt behind and learn to trust Christ through our daily activities.

Consider how we are invited to grow in our knowledge of Him through the renewing of our mind.

"Grow in the grace and knowledge of our Lord and Savior Jesus Christ."

2 Peter 3:18 (NIV)

"Do not conform to the pattern of this world, but be transformed by the renewing of your mind."

Romans 12:2 (NIV)

Renewing our mind is a process that begins with repentance and belief, and then continues through the act of following Christ. It involves the replacement of our doubt with Christ's truth.

Throughout Scripture, we are continually invited to repent (change our minds) and believe (change our hearts) by placing our faith and trust in His ways over our ways.

Transformation does not occur through academic adherence but through personal experience. It is not just about knowing about God or knowing what God says, it is about learning to know and trust God through a personal relationship with Him.

When we follow Christ, He leads us and guides us through experiential learning that teaches us that He is trustworthy. Paul references this process of being "trained" throughout his letters. Following is the training ground in which we learn to replace our weak doubts and misbeliefs with the strength of God's eternal truths.

As we follow, our understanding is replaced with His understanding, and the patterns that guided our life in the past, are replaced with His plans as we follow His direction for our lives.

"For my thoughts are not your thoughts, neither are your ways my ways," declares the Lord."

Isaiah 55:8 (NIV)

When we understand, embrace, and apply the invitations to repent, believe, and follow, to our daily lives, we begin to move forward in faith, trusting that God will continue to reveal, guide, and sustain us in the directions that He is leading us.

This is the key to Christ-centered living.

This is why we are told that the *"righteous will live by faith"* (Romans 1:17, Galatians 3:11, Hebrews 10:38).

Faith is Not a Magic Wand That We Use to Control God

Sometimes the concept of faith or belief is used to mislead and abuse Christians into foolish activities based on human emotions and manipulation.

For example, some teach that all we need to do is "name and claim" something and then God, much like a genie in a bottle, will rise up and serve us.

This view is a misunderstanding of our relationship with God, as well as a misapplication of the concept of faith. Faith is not a tool to control God or to ensure that He meets our needs.

If "naming and claiming" is a theologically accurate application of mature faith, then certainly the apostle Paul would not only have been able to heal himself, but he would not have had to work as a tentmaker or request funding and support from local churches to spread the gospel (2 Corinthians 12:7).

Faith is meaningless unless it is placed in something reliable and reasonable.

Our faith is not in ourselves.

We are unreliable.

God is unchanging.

We cannot know what is reliable and reasonable unless we follow Christ through studying the Word of God. In so doing, we put down roots. It is how we learn to know the truth in order for the truth to set us free.

Jesus understood the road ahead. He knew His disciples were at risk of being scorched if not properly rooted in knowledge that would lead them toward reasoned confident beliefs.

> *"In this world you will have trouble, but take heart! I have overcome the world."*
>
> *John 16:33 (NIV)*

We would be wise to take heed and listen to the admonition of Solomon:

> *"Remember your Creator in the days of your youth, before the days of trouble come."*
>
> *Ecclesiastes 12:1 (NIV)*

In order to navigate the inevitable days of trouble that are ahead, we must learn to hear and identify God's voice so we can learn to follow securely behind Him.

> *"My sheep hear My voice, and I know them, and they follow Me; and I give eternal life to them, and they will never perish; and no one will snatch them out of My hand."*
>
> *John 10:27-28 (NASB)*

Who Among Us

Who among us does not wrestle with fears and unknowns?

Who among us is not tempted to trust our ways rather than God's?

Who among us is not guilty of rationalizing our lack of belief?

Our first step toward a true, reasoned, and confident belief that directs our hearts away from self-trust and self-centered living is to change our mind about God's willingness to hear and accept our struggles with unbelief.

Our next step is to leave our doubt behind as we learn to accept Christ's invitation to trust and follow Him.

To do so, we must take the bold and courageous step of asking Him to help us with our unbelief.

God desires to fill you and to lavish you with all you need for life and for Christ-like reflection (2 Peter 1:3); but, you and I must dare to respond. Otherwise we risk shrinking back into the timidity of unreasoned faith.

In our struggle to believe, we must confess our unbelief and ask the Father who loves to give good gifts to His children to meet us in our moment of weakness (Matthew 7:11, 1 John 3:1).

Then we must walk forward in active faith by putting legs to our belief and accepting Christ's invitation to follow Him, learning to trust that God is rich in grace to those who confess their need to rely more fully on Him.

In the moments that we struggle with doubt, we need to receive the grace filled words found in Jude 1:22, "Be merciful to those who doubt," with confidence (NIV).

In our moments of failure, we can renew our minds with the truth about our standing in grace. We can continue to walk forward confidently, claiming God's promise through Paul that *"there is no condemnation of those who are in Christ Jesus" (Romans 8:1).*

Growing more rooted in truth gives us the freedom to approach Him honestly and without shame.

In this way, Jesus not only invites us to imitate Him, but to receive healing from Him and to build our lives around His truth as we continue to train ourselves to become His reflections (1 Timothy 4:7-8 NIV).

With each and every step we take, our rabbi continues to teach us to trust that

> *"The steadfast love of the Lord never ceases; his mercies never come to an end; they are new every morning; great is your faithfulness."*
> Lamentations 3:22-23 (ESV)

Notes and Discussion

"So then, just as you received Christ Jesus as Lord, continue to live in him, rooted and built up in him, strengthened in the faith as you were taught, and overflowing with thankfulness. See to it that no one takes you captive through hollow and deceptive philosophy, which depends on human tradition and the basic principles of this world rather than on Christ. For in Christ all the fullness of the Deity lives in bodily form, and you have been given fullness in Christ, who is the head over every power and authority."

Colossians 2:6-10 (NIV)

"Therefore, as you received Christ Jesus the Lord, so walk in him, rooted and built up in him and established in the faith, just as you were taught, abounding in thanksgiving. See to it that no one takes you captive by philosophy and empty deceit, according to human tradition, according to the elemental spirits of the world, and not according to Christ. For in him the whole fullness of deity dwells bodily, and you have been filled in him, who is the head of all rule and authority."

Colossians 2:6-10 (ESV)

Memory Verse Study

Beginning with Colossians 2:6-10, describe the process of following Christ.

Verse overview:

Passage study:

Concept study:

"Therefore, I urge you, brothers, in view of God's mercy, to offer your bodies as living sacrifices, holy and pleasing to God—this is your spiritual act of worship. Do not conform any longer to the pattern of this world, but be transformed by the renewing of your mind. Then you will be able to test and approve what God's will is—his good, pleasing and perfect will."

Romans 12:1-2 (NIV)

"I appeal to you therefore, brothers, by the mercies of God, to present your bodies as a living sacrifice, holy and acceptable to God, which is your spiritual worship. Do not be conformed to this world, but be transformed by the renewal of your mind, that by testing you may discern what is the will of God, what is good and acceptable and perfect."

Romans 12:1-2 (ESV)

Memory Verse Study

Beginning with Romans 12:1-2, describe the process of transformation.

Verse overview:

Passage study:

Concept study:

Concept study

What is the process of training that Christ used to equip His followers? Why?

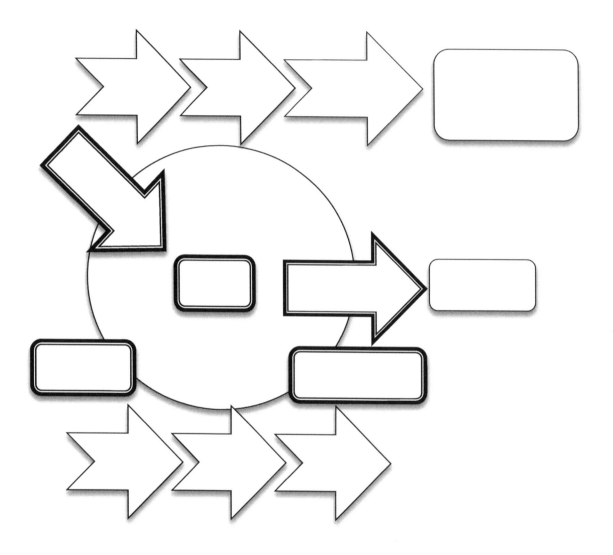

What is the purpose of spiritual disciplines?

Notes and Discussion

"Why do John's disciples fast?"
            - Mark 2:18

1. What are spiritual disciplines?

2. What are the purpose of spiritual disciplines?

3. How can they be misused?

4. How can they be applied effectively?

5. What is the motivation for spiritual disciplines?

6. What is the power source for spiritual disciplines?

What is prayer?

Notes and Discussion

"Lord, teach us to pray."

- Luke 11:1-13

Love & Deny

Spiritual Formation

Unit Essential Questions

1. How does Christ's invitation to love Him and deny ourselves apply to my life?

2. Where are the areas in my life that I need to learn to trust Jesus?

Unit Learning Objectives

A. To understand the difference between a cause and outcome in the process of growing to become a friend of Jesus

B. To examine the spiritual needs and obstacles of trust, worry, and self that exist at this stage in the journey of reflecting Christ

C. To examine the process of time, trials, temptations, and trust in developing our perseverance and completing the work of maturity in our lives

Unit Learning Assessments

1. Reading: *Respond: Christ-Centered Discipleship* Philippians, 1 Peter

2. Memorization: James 1:2-4, Hebrews 12:1-3

3. Socratic Dialogue: Philippians, 1 Peter Journal and Community Discussion

4. Trials, Temptations and Trust Reflection Paper

Daily Essential Questions

1. What is the difference between being a follower and being a friend of Jesus?

2. What is the difference between a transformative cause and outcome?

3. How does Jesus use testing and trials as a part of the transformation process?

4. How does God use trials, temptations, and time to teach trust?

5. What is the role of community and accountability in transformation?

6. How do I live with joy in the midst of trials?

"Consider it pure joy, my brothers and sisters, whenever you face trials of many kinds, because you know that the testing of your faith produces perseverance. Let perseverance finish its work so that you may be mature and complete, not lacking anything."

James 1:2-4 (NIV)

"Count it all joy, my brothers, when you meet trials of various kinds, for you know that the testing of your faith produces steadfastness. And let steadfastness have its full effect, that you may be perfect and complete, lacking in nothing."

James 1:2-4 (ESV)

Concept study

What is the difference between being a follower and becoming a friend of Jesus?

Understanding the Bible memory verse: James 1:2-4

What does it say?

What does it mean?

How do obstacles help me grow?

The spiritual growth obstacles at this stage are the weeds: trials, temptations, worries, cares of this world, and finances. The temptation appears wherever we place our trust.

Application: What is the process that everyone needs to go through in order to move from a follower to a friend of Jesus?

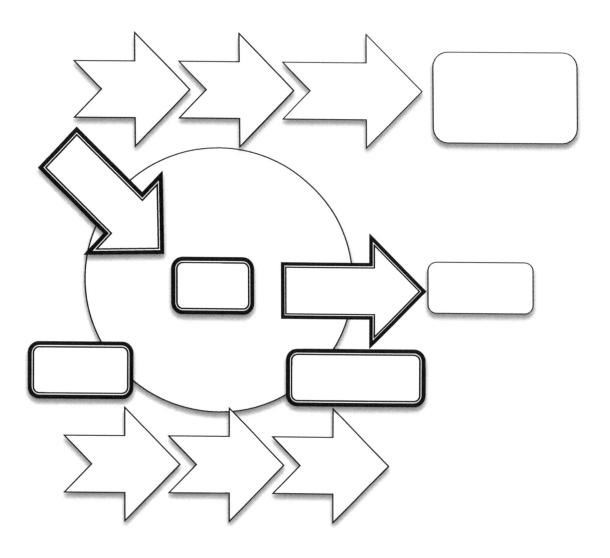

"Therefore, since we are surrounded by such a great cloud of witnesses, let us throw off everything that hinders and the sin that so easily entangles. And let us run with perseverance the race marked out for us, fixing our eyes on Jesus, the pioneer and perfecter of faith. For the joy set before him he endured the cross, scorning its shame, and sat down at the right hand of the throne of God. Consider him who endured such opposition from sinners, so that you will not grow weary and lose heart."

Hebrews 12:1-3 (NIV)

"Therefore, since we are surrounded by so great a cloud of witnesses, let us also lay aside every weight, and sin which clings so closely, and let us run with endurance the race that is set before us, looking to Jesus, the founder and perfecter of our faith, who for the joy that was set before him endured the cross, despising the shame, and is seated at the right hand of the throne of God. Consider him who endured from sinners such hostility against himself, so that you may not grow weary or fainthearted."

Hebrews 12:1-3 (ESV)

Concept study

What is the difference between focusing on a cause and focusing on an outcome of spiritual growth and how does that apply to this stage?

Understanding the Bible memory verse: Hebrews 12:1-3

What does it say?

What does it mean?

Application: How is Jesus the hero of this stage? Explain your answer.

Love & Deny
Notes and Discussion

Love & Deny
Notes and Discussion

Essential Question

How is God at work in my life through the process of trials and temptations?

Learning Goal

To apply personal examination and reflection to demonstrate understanding and application of the concepts of trials and spiritual maturity

Part I. Personal Reflection

Answer the following three questions.

1. How is God at work in my life through the process of trials and temptations to invite me toward the goal of spiritual maturity?

    "For physical training is of some value, but godliness has value for all things, holding promise for both the present life and the life to come" (1 Timothy 4:8).

    "But solid food is for the mature, who by constant use have trained themselves to distinguish good from evil" (Hebrews 5:14).

    "No discipline seems pleasant at the time, but painful. Later on, however, it produces a harvest of righteousness and peace for those who have been trained by it" (Hebrews 12:11).

    B. What has been my response to the trial or temptation, up to this point?

    C. How is God in the process of renewing my mind toward the trial or temptation?

    "Do not conform any longer to the pattern of this world, but be transformed by the renewing of your mind. Then you will be able to test and approve what God's will is—his good, pleasing and perfect will" (Romans 12:2).

Part II. Application

Situation: After reflecting on your own life. Consider a situation where you are discipling someone else who is struggling to move from being a follower of Jesus to a friend of Jesus.

As part of their growth process, you learn that they are experiencing trials and temptations..
A. What will you tell them?

B. Why?

C. What Scripture would you use to back up your responses?

In your paper, make sure to address the concepts of spiritual needs, obstacles to growth, and the process of moving from knowing God to loving God. (Time, trials/temptations, trust, love/deny, obey, friend).

Go. Teach

Spiritual Formation

INVITED TO FOLLOW

Unit Essential Questions

1. How does Christ's invitation to go and teach apply to my life?

2. Where are my circles of influence in which I am called to reflect Christ?

Unit Learning Objectives

A. To demonstrate understanding and application of what it means, in my life, that Jesus commissioned me to go and reproduce the process of learning to reflect Him by sharing my spiritual journey with others.

Unit Learning Assessments

1. Spiritual Equipping Project and Presentation

Daily Essential Questions

1. How do I share with others what God is doing in my life?

2. What is God doing in and through the lives of my classmates?

3. What are my next steps for growth?

"And the things you have heard me say in the presence of many witnesses entrust to reliable men who will also be qualified to teach others."
2 Timothy 2:2 (NIV)

"And what you have heard from me in the presence of many witnesses entrust to faithful men who will be able to teach others also."
2 Timothy 2:2 (ESV)

Go. Teach
Notes and Discussion

Go. Teach
Notes and Discussion

Resources

Spiritual Formation

INVITED TO FOLLOW

How to write a one-page paper for Bible class: APA Format

It is not enough to simply memorize Bible facts or acquire biblical knowledge. Students need to be given the opportunity to wrestle with important issues, develop personal beliefs, and articulate those beliefs in clear and convincing ways in both written and oral form. At our school, we value the abilities to think critically and communicate clearly about theological truth. It is the belief of the Bible department that Bible class offers the opportunity to practice and develop these skills through the medium of one-page papers.

One-page papers are made up of a centered title and four critical paragraphs. The first part of the paper is referred to as the "hook" paragraph and it is used to relate the topic to the audience. The second part of the paper is the "book" paragraph. The purpose of this paragraph is to clearly state the main concept of the paper. The third paragraph is the "look" paragraph and it is where the author illustrates the main point that they outlined in the second paragraph. The fourth or final section is called the "took" paragraph. It is in this final paragraph the author outlines a personal application, lesson, or "take away" from the topic.

Each individual paragraph must also contain a few key elements. One of the key elements is that each paragraph needs a minimum of four sentences. Another key element is that each paragraph needs to include transition sentences and be double-spaced. The paper is also written using either 11- or 12-point Times New Roman or Arial font. Finally, while the paper itself will use APA guidelines, it is important to note that the paper must not be longer than one page in total length (Bible Reference 1:1).

There are three main things that I need to learn through these papers. First, I will have critically examined my personal beliefs. Second, I will have learned how to communicate my beliefs in concise written form. Third and finally, I will have a collection of papers outlining my beliefs to use for personal reference in the future.

How to Write a One-Paged Paper for Bible Class: MLA Format

It is not enough to simply memorize Bible facts or acquire biblical knowledge. Students need to be given the opportunity to wrestle with important issues, develop personal beliefs, and articulate those beliefs in clear and convincing ways in both written and oral form. The abilities to think critically and communicate clearly about theological truth are becoming increasingly valuable. Bible class offers the opportunity to practice and develop these skills through the medium of one-page papers.

One-page papers should closely resemble this paper – following all MLA standards – consisting of a centered title and four critical paragraphs. The first paragraph is the "hook" (Intro) paragraph and is used to relate the topic and provide a thesis statement. The second paragraph is the "book" (Body 1) paragraph. This paragraph is to clearly explain the main concept of the paper. The third paragraph is the "look" (Body 2) paragraph and is where the author illustrates his/her main point regarding what is outlined in the second paragraph. The fourth paragraph is called the "took" (conclusion) paragraph. In this paragraph, the author outlines a personal application, lesson, or "take away" from the topic.

Each individual paragraph must contain a few key elements. One, each paragraph needs a minimum of four sentences, and two, each paragraph needs to include transitional sentences. The paper is also written using either 11-point Arial or 12-point Times New Roman font. Use parenthetical citations when necessary with the following format: (biblical reference, translation) e.g., (Gen.1:1, NIV). Finally, it is important to note that the paper must not be longer than one page in total length (approximately 350 words) and be double spaced. There is no need for any fluff. The paper must be concise and precise.

There are three main things that the author needs to learn through these papers. First, the author will have critically examined his/her personal beliefs. Second, the author will have learned how to communicate his/her beliefs in concise written form. Third, the author will have a collection of papers outlining his/her beliefs for personal reference in the future.

"Therefore be imitators of God, as beloved children."
Ephesians 5:1 (NASB)

"Therefore be imitators of God, as beloved children."
Ephesians 5:1 (ESV)

"For the word of God is living and active. Sharper than any double-edged sword, it penetrates even to dividing soul and spirit, joints and marrow; it judges the thoughts and attitudes of the heart."
Hebrews 4:12 (NIV)

"For the word of God is living and active, sharper than any two-edged sword, piercing to the division of soul and of spirit, of joints and of marrow, and discerning the thoughts and intentions of the heart."
Hebrews 4:12 (ESV)

"All Scripture is God-breathed and is useful for teaching, rebuking, correcting and training in righteousness, so that the man of God may be thoroughly equipped for every good work."
2 Timothy 3:16-17 (NIV)

"All Scripture is breathed out by God and profitable for teaching, for reproof, for correction, and for training in righteousness, that the man of God may be competent, equipped for every good work."
2 Timothy 3:16-17 (ESV)

"Do your best to present yourself to God as one approved, a workman who does not need to be ashamed and who correctly handles the word of truth."
2 Timothy 2:15 (NIV)

"Do your best to present yourself to God as one approved, a worker who has no need to be ashamed, rightly handling the word of truth."
2 Timothy 2:15 (ESV)

"Do you not know that in a race all the runners run, but only one gets the prize? Run in such a way as to get the prize. Everyone who competes in the games goes into strict training. They do it to get a crown that will not last; but we do it to get a crown that will last forever. Therefore I do not run like a man running aimlessly; I do not fight like a man beating the air."
1 Corinthians 9:24-26 (NIV)

"Do you not know that in a race all the runners run, but only one receives the prize? So run that you may obtain it. Every athlete exercises self-control in all things. They do it to receive a perishable wreath, but we an imperishable. So I do not run aimlessly; I do not box as one beating the air."
1 Corinthians 9:24-26 (ESV)

"The Word became flesh and made his dwelling among us. We have seen his glory, the glory of the One and Only, who came from the Father, full of grace and truth."
John 1:14 (NIV)

"And the Word became flesh and dwelt among us, and we have seen his glory, glory as of the only Son from the Father, full of grace and truth."
John 1:14 (ESV)

"For God so loved the world that he gave his one and only Son, that whoever believes in him shall not perish but have eternal life. For God did not send his Son into the world to condemn the world, but to save the world through him."

John 3:16-17(NIV)

"For God so loved the world, that he gave his only Son, that whoever believes in him should not perish but have eternal life. For God did not send his Son into the world to condemn the world, but in order that the world might be saved through him."

John 3:16-17 (ESV)

"Now, brothers, I want to remind you of the Gospel I preached to you, which you received and on which you have taken your stand. By this Gospel you are saved, if you hold firmly to the word I preached to you. Otherwise, you have believed in vain. For what I received I passed on to you as of first importance: that Christ died for our sins according to the Scriptures, that he was buried, that he was raised on the third day according to the Scriptures, and that he appeared to Peter, and then to the Twelve. After that, he appeared to more than five hundred of the brothers at the same time, most of whom are still living, though some have fallen asleep."

I Corinthians 15:1-6 (NIV)

"Now I would remind you, brothers, of the Gospel I preached to you, which you received, in which you stand, and by which you are being saved, if you hold fast to the word I preached to you—unless you believed in vain. For I delivered to you as of first importance what I also received: that Christ died for our sins in accordance with the Scriptures, that he was buried, that he was raised on the third day in accordance with the Scriptures, and that he appeared to Peter, then to the twelve. Then he appeared to more than five hundred brothers at one time, most of whom are still alive, though some have fallen asleep."

I Corinthians 15:1-6 (ESV)

"Therefore, I urge you, brothers, in view of God's mercy, to offer your bodies as living sacrifices, holy and pleasing to God—this is your spiritual act of worship. Do not conform any longer to the pattern of this world, but be transformed by the renewing of your mind. Then you will be able to test and approve what God's will is—his good, pleasing and perfect will."

Romans 12:1-2 (NIV)

"I appeal to you therefore, brothers, by the mercies of God, to present your bodies as a living sacrifice, holy and acceptable to God, which is your spiritual worship. Do not be conformed to this world, but be transformed by the renewal of your mind, that by testing you may discern what is the will of God, what is good and acceptable and perfect."

Romans 12:1-2 (ESV)

"So then, just as you received Christ Jesus as Lord, continue to live in him, rooted and built up in him, strengthened in the faith as you were taught, and overflowing with thankfulness.
See to it that no one takes you captive through hollow and deceptive philosophy, which depends on human tradition and the basic principles of this world rather than on Christ. For in Christ all the fullness of the Deity lives in bodily form, and you have been given fullness in Christ, who is the head over every power and authority."

Colossians 2:6-10 (NIV)

"Therefore, as you received Christ Jesus the Lord, so walk in him, rooted and built up in him and established in the faith, just as you were taught, abounding in thanksgiving. See to it that no one takes you captive by philosophy and empty deceit, according to human tradition, according to the elemental spirits of the world, and not according to Christ. For in him the whole fullness of deity dwells bodily, and you have been filled in him, who is the head of all rule and authority."

Colossians 2:6-10 (ESV)

"Consider it pure joy, my brothers and sisters, whenever you face trials of many kinds, because you know that the testing of your faith produces perseverance. Let perseverance finish its work so that you may be mature and complete, not lacking anything."

James 1:2-4 (NIV)

"Count it all joy, my brothers, when you meet trials of various kinds, for you know that the testing of your faith produces steadfastness. And let steadfastness have its full effect, that you may be perfect and complete, lacking in nothing."

James 1:2-4 (ESV)

"Therefore, since we are surrounded by such a great cloud of witnesses, let us throw off everything that hinders and the sin that so easily entangles. And let us run with perseverance the race marked out for us, fixing our eyes on Jesus, the pioneer and perfecter of faith. For the joy set before him he endured the cross, scorning its shame, and sat down at the right hand of the throne of God. Consider him who endured such opposition from sinners, so that you will not grow weary and lose heart."

Hebrews 12:1-3 (NIV)

"Therefore, since we are surrounded by so great a cloud of witnesses, let us also lay aside every weight, and sin which clings so closely, and let us run with endurance the race that is set before us, looking to Jesus, the founder and perfecter of our faith, who for the joy that was set before him endured the cross, despising the shame, and is seated at the right hand of the throne of God. Consider him who endured from sinners such hostility against himself, so that you may not grow weary or fainthearted."

Hebrews 12:1-3 (ESV)